Quiet Spy Secret War

The Life and Times of James William Lair in Thailand, Laos and Texas

By M H Burton

2019

Introduction

Few people know the name of the CIA's most successful Vietnam War Era agent. During his spying career his picture never appeared in any American newspaper or magazine; or any foreign one for that matter. He was never interviewed on television. Was never called to testify before Congress. Was never publicly acknowledged as a hero by anyone, including the CIA. His name never appeared on the anti-war leftists' lengthy lists of American mass murderers, war criminals, drug traffickers, war profiteers, and evil masterminds. As nothing ever dies on the Internet you can find those lists and the charges brought against men like Allen Dulles, John McCone, William Colby, Richard Secord, Theodore Shackley, William H. Sullivan, General Vang Pao, and Edgar "Pop" Buell still as fresh there as if they had been posted yesterday. All those men were this man's associates; some of them were good friends, others were enemies, still others were by turns friends and enemies.

How could the CIA's most successful agent not have been outed when all those others were? And just what did he do that made him so successful? This biography of James William "Bill" Lair answers both questions. It's a long story. A story that takes as many twists and turns as a good spy novel. But it's not fiction. It all happened. And Bill Lair was at the center of it all.

Table of Contents

Part VI: A Brief Exile and a "Special" Return 1968-76

Part VII: An Uneasy Retirement 1976-92

Part VIII: Return of the Ancient Agent 1992-2014

LAIR COUNTRY

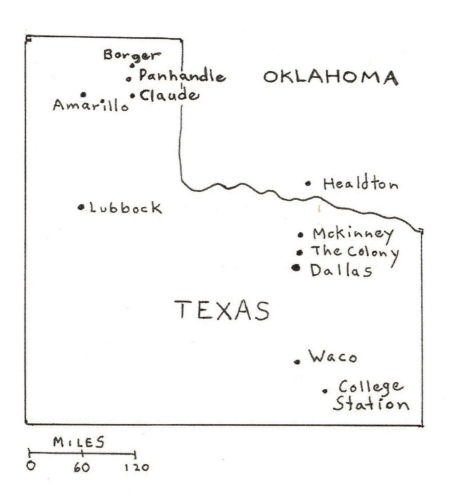

Part I: A Man of Humble Birth - 1924-42

Chapter 1: Off to a Bad Start

James William (Bill) Lair (1924-2014) was born in or around Healdton, OK (pronounced "Hilton" by locals), 20 miles north of the border of the Texas Panhandle. It has a population of 2800 today. Settled in 1887 as a cotton growing area, it became an oil boomtown in 1914. Healdton doesn't list Bill as one of its "notable" people. The only person on that list is actress Rue McClanahan. His father was Charles Price (Charley) Lair (1898-1974). His mother Lehta Mae Lair (nee Tompkins) (1903-91). They were married in 1923. Bill was their first born and only son. He had two sisters, Charlene (1925-83) and Narcill (1927-2012).

Lehta's marriage was a disaster. Charley Price Lair was a handsome irresponsible loafer who didn't support his wife and children. The last-born child of William Hardin Lair (1873-1958) and Sudie Tye (1876-1898) who died giving birth to him. Taken at birth by his maternal grandmother Lee Ellen Scroggins Tye (1848-?) he was raised as an only child and spoiled rotten. She changed his last name to Tye, but he later changed it back to Lair. Spent his whole adult life hanging around the Healdton area rarely working and sponging off friends and relatives. Had nothing to do with any of his children after Lehta left him in 1927. Also had nothing to do with his own father. Didn't even attend his funeral. Bill described his father as "handsome and well-liked, but he never took anything seriously. Never worked. Never wanted to work." Quoted his mother saying she left him because "If I continued to live with him, I've already got three kids, we're always going to be just one jump ahead of the popper, never able to send the kids to school. I'm not going to do that. I'm going to get rid of him and I'm going to do it myself."

She took her three youngsters and moved back home to her father, James A. (Jim) Tompkins (1877?-1937) in the hamlet of Hewitt not far from Healdton joining her mother Florence (1882-1952) and seven brothers and sisters (two more were yet to be born) in 1927. Jim Tompkins was a blacksmith who'd had a shop in the village of Sugden, OK when Lehta was born but moved his business closer to Healdton when it boomed. They all moved to the oil boomtown of Borger, Texas in 1928. Once there Lehta divorced Charley and remarried, though there is no record of either a divorce or a second marriage. That would not be unusual in a town as chaotic, violent and lawless as 1930s Borger. The man she married was Frank L. Swaffar (1892-1937) a WWI veteran and oil field worker. Frank died spectacularly on April 20, 1937. A pressure tank at the Danube Oil Corporation's refinery exploded while he was trying to douse a blaze there. He had been passing by the refinery on his way to work at nearby oil rig and joined the fire fighting. His skull was crushed, and a leg broken. As if Lehta's "man trouble" wasn't already bad enough her father also died in 1937. She received a modest death benefit from Frank's insurance policy which she later used to take an accounting course.

So how violent and lawless was Bloody Borger? It didn't even exist until 1921 when Gulf Oil brought in the first gusher in the Panhandle. Named after Ace Borger, an early wildcatter who not only made a fortune in oil but controlled the local lumber business and brickyard. How could a town named after someone nicknamed "Ace" possibly be a quiet and peaceful community? More gushers soon followed the first one, by 1926 800 wells had been drilled at Borger. 45,000 people, most of them men, crowded into the place. They lived in tents and tarpaper shacks on dirt roads, breathed in wind-blown dust and soot from the carbon black plants. The whole town was encrusted in dust and soot. A vicious town full of cardsharps, prostitutes, bootleggers and opium dens. A town where murders, robberies and 'disappearances' were everyday occurrences. A town visually memorialized by Thomas Hart Benton's mural-sized painting "Boomtown" (1923). Rooms rented for $50-$100 a month (more than ten times that in today's dollars). Each bed was shared by three men who had it for one 8-hour shift. The criminal element was so numerous that the town "jail" consisted of a log where up to 80 miscreants, both men and women, were chained until they paid fines to be released. Fines were the town's main source of revenue. Borger's first sheriff was Two-gun Dick Herwig, a convicted murderer from Oklahoma who took bribes, pimped whores, taxed moonshiners, and collected protection money from legitimate businesses. Those who didn't pay up were beaten up, or murdered, by his thuggish "deputies".

In 1927 the Governor of Texas sent Texas Rangers to clean up the town. They cleaned it up, briefly. Gave prostitutes 'till sundown to get out of town. The "girls" marched off toward Amarillo in a column a mile long. Most returned as soon as the Rangers left. Then things got back to "normal" in Borger and chaos once again reigned supreme. The Rangers, reinforced by 84 Texas State Guardsmen, returned in 1929 and jailed the entire local police force. The Governor of Texas put the town under martial law for 30 days, but once again 'Bloody Borger' quickly reverted to its old vile self. In 1934 Ace Borger was gunned down while mailing a letter at the post office. The bullet that passed through his body also killed an innocent bystander. Only a sharp fall in the price of oil in the late 30's tamed wild and wooly Borger. But by then the widowed Lehta Shaffar and her brood, who still bore the name Lair, were gone. "People disappeared every day in Borger" Bill remarked. No wonder WWII and the Secret War in Laos didn't faze him.

Now back to Lehta's story. The double deaths left her without means of support. In that same year of 1937 she moved to Panhandle, Texas, another oil boomtown, 25 miles away from Borger. A boomtown that had already gone bust due to cratering crude prices caused by slack demand and overproduction. Panhandle was much smaller than Borger and, with the oil bust, much more peaceful. Once there she became head of a household that included her three children, her mother, and her mother's three youngest children. They found a cheap ($12 a month) place to live in a house at an abandoned "Oil Camp" owned by Phillips Petroleum. Oil camps were built by the oil companies to house employees, mainly men, who worked wells in the surrounding area. The oil companies still owned the "Camps" and were happy to rent them out to anyone who would pay a few bucks for the housing so that it would be occupied until a hoped-for oil boom returned. (One did return in 1941 with WWII).

With the Great Depression still in full swing in 1937 there were plenty of folks needing dirt cheap lodging. The Oil Camp, which was just a few miles from Panhandle, was full up. So many young children that one of the buildings was turned into a one room country school. Young Bill Lair, who had hated Borger, loved Panhandle. He recounted an informal Indian artifact hunt in Borger with several fellow boy scouts that turned up a skeleton. The boys thought it was an Indian. Later found out that it was a murder victim planted there four years before. But Panhandle was different. His family was poor, but they were surrounded by other families who were just as poor. Almost nobody had any money in Panhandle. Poor honest folks. The criminal element had decamped with the oil.

"Everybody knew everybody else in Panhandle" you could almost see him smiling as he said that. He walked to dear old PHS every school day. A small school, just four teachers, including the Principal and his wife. There were 25 students in his Junior Year class. His favorite subjects were History and English and he did very well in Math. Played football and basketball...and worked after school to help support his family. Learned the printing trade working at the weekly *Panhandle Herald.* It came out on Friday. He spent every Thursday night running the linotype machine and assisting the printer. Took a two-hour morning snooze and went off to Friday classes. Worked Saturdays setting up commercial printing jobs. Was paid three dollars a week. Asked for a raise and the publisher told him he should be glad that he was learning a useful trade. He wasn't that glad, so he quit and went to work for a grocery store that paid five dollars a week. Worked so much that his grades suffered. Lehta was worried and asked the Principal about him. Was told that he was the smartest kid in his class; that anyone that smart and that hard-working would do well in life. The family's only other income was from his mother's work as housekeeper at an old people's home. But smart, well-educated, tough-minded Lehta wasn't going to let life get her down. She'd gone to Normal School (Teachers College) for two years after graduating

Healdton HS. Married shiftless Charley instead of becoming a teacher. Bad choice, but she was determined to recover from its consequences.

Lehta parlayed her accounting training into a job as a Finance Officer in the Accounting Department at the Headquarters of the Veterans Administration in Waco. When computers eliminated her job in 1960, she passed an exam and was retrained as a paralegal at the University of Houston, then worked in the VA's Legal Department until she retired in 1969. Bill was sad to leave Panhandle. Wanted to graduate with the PHS class of '41, but knows Waco is a good move for the family. He spends his senior year at Waco High School, graduating with the Class of 1941 at the age of just under 17. His mother wants him to go to college. He wants to go to Texas A & M University at College Station, 50 miles from Waco. She has a new, much better job, but they are still struggling financially. He decides to get a job and earn at least enough money to cover tuition and board and room at A & M. Goes to a local printing company and shows them the skills he learned at the *Panhandle Herald*. They snap him up. Works for them from June '41 'till December. Then enrolls at A & M. Pearl Harbor's attacked before he can start classes. Looks like he won't have a chance to complete, or even get a good start, on his college education. The Draft begins to crank up. He's only 17 so he doesn't have to register for it until his 18th birthday. He completes his one college semester, then goes after as much cash as he can get, back to now-booming Borger to work in the oil fields.

Bill later (at age 86) paints a patriotic picture of his WWII entry. Says he joined the Army "not long after Pearl Harbor" that he was anxious to go, afraid he'd miss his chance to fight. Says he had to get permission from his mother to enlist at 17. Says he tried to get into Navy pilot school but was turned down for poor eyesight. An earlier interview at age 77 contradicts this inspiring story. The facts support the uninspiring version. The Navy Pilot part is half-right. While at A & M he tries to get into a Navy program that is somewhat like the Vietnam War era ROTC. He would receive Navy Officer training while attending college. So long as he stays in the program he's exempted from the draft and can continue in college. "Same program later-President George H. W. Bush, a fellow Texan, was in at Yale" he points out.

Bill passed the physical but failed the eye exam. He enlisted in the Army on 3 December 1942, nearly a year after Pearl Harbor. Worked the Borger oil fields until then. Visited an Army recruiter during the late summer with the Draft breathing down his neck. Inquired about enlistment opportunities. Recruiter steered him toward armored. Said it was about to become a new Army Corps. He shows interest but later enlists in the infantry.

Chapter 2: Role Models

Now that I have laid out the bare facts, it's time to get on to the guts of James William Lair's childhood and young adulthood. He certainly had a rough go of it. No effective father. Moves at least 4 times before he graduates high school. Grows up in poverty either living with relatives, or in a single parent household headed by his mother, or with a stepfather who is quickly vaporized. Always renting. Family owns nothing.

So how did he survive such a rotten childhood? His Wikipedia bio mentions "Lair's grandfather, an old-time cowboy, was an important influence on Bill's life"; but contains no details. That man was William Harlan Lair (1873-1958) usually known as "W H", his paternal grandfather. Bill lived with him for two years, also spent 'two or three summers' with him between 1930 and 1937. They stayed in contact off and on until his death in 1958. W H was indeed an "old-time cowboy". His family had come to Texas from Kentucky in 1857 settling in the McKinney area. As a young man he worked for the Matador Land and Cattle Company as a ranch hand. Later managed a remote hay farm for Charlie Goodnight, owner of the sprawling Goodnight Ranch. A sociable man he tired of managing a spread that was "25 miles away from anything" so he quit and bought a modest ranch near Claude, TX where he and his second wife...a widower married to a widow, ran a small outfit that wasn't much more than a subsistence farm. Raised a few horses and cattle, some hogs and chickens. Planted a few acres of cotton as a cash crop. Bill remembers him as a great man with horses. "We had almost no money, but we always ate well, and worked hard. He took me around with him and treated me like an adult. Was good at working with other people. Taught me how to do it, and how important it was to be good at it. Had only a 4th Grade education but he was plenty smart". There were other adult men around the Lair Ranch too. Bill's Uncle Tullus "Bud" Lair (1897-1968), and Paul Lair (1907-73). Paul was the son of W H's second wife Josie (1883-?). Both men were lifelong bachelors. "Bud" rarely spoke but worked hard. Paul was more voluble, also a hard worker. They all worked hard, including young Bill. "I learned how to be a CIA case officer from my Grandpa. How to work in the field and deal with agents. He liked people. Was able to work with all kinds of people. Got along with everybody and was able to talk them into doing things."

The other steadying influence in his life was his mother. Her own life started out promising. She graduated from Healdton OK High School in 1920 at age 16. One of the three top students in her class, perhaps the smartest of the three. Straight A's in their senior year...all girls of course. Their cameo pictures featured in the yearbook. The other two girls could be considered "cute" by 1920 standards. Hair stylishly bobbed, posing selfie-like for the camera. Lehta Mae Tompkins was not "cute". A round face suggests plumpness. A large flattened nose. Wild unkempt hair. A serious expression. Staring wide-eyed at the lens. The yearbook gushes over the great prospects of HHS's three brightest students. Lehta starts out on the right foot. Goes to Normal College preparing for a teaching career. Then marries a handsome deadbeat who gave her three quick children in four years that she, or rather she and her father Jim Tompkins, ended up having to support. She encouraged young Bill to study hard. She wanted him to succeed in life. He had her brains in addition to her encouragement. A shy, bookish, diffident boy. A voracious reader with wide ranging interests. Quiet, self-effacing and soft-spoken, a deep thinker. A good listener and a keen observer of what was going on around him. He got those traits from her, and his grandfather. He didn't get them from Charley Lair. He inherited his mother's brains and his father's body. 20-year-old Charley's 1918 draft registration card lists him as 5-9 and 175 pounds. Several pictures show him good looking and well put together. 18-year-old Bill's 1942 Army enlistment records say he is 5-9 and 149. Charley's pampered childhood and aversion to work no doubt left him better fed than Bill. He looks a lot like his father, but he has his mother's eyes. Those serious probing eyes.

Bill never had anything to do with his deadbeat father, and his father never had anything to do with him or his two sisters. Still he showed no strong resentment toward him. "That's just the way he was. There were many others around like him in those days" he remarked. Being able to accept people "the way they were" is another trait that served him well as a CIA agent. He kept in close touch with his mother for the rest of her long life. She was the only person he wrote letters to during his four years in the Army. He arranged two extended visits for her to Thailand and spoke with pride of how fascinated she was with the Kingdom and how well she was accepted by his upper-crust Thai wife and in-laws. He never forgot her.

Part II: A Quiet Man Goes to War - 1942-45

Chapter 3: Joining Up

"In late '40 or early '41 I went to a lecture in the basement of the First Christian Church in Waco by a man, I think he was a Jew, but I'm not sure. Anyway, he was a German, and he had been arrested by the Gestapo and jailed for a long time, treated badly in jail. Later escaped to Russia and was picked up by the Secret Service there and they treated him even worse than the Gestapo did. Escaped from them and made his way to Italy and from there to the US. He told us that we'd have to fight Hitler even if we didn't want to now, but that Hitler's Master Race Theory wasn't going to work because the world wouldn't stand for it. That we'd eventually beat his Third Reich. Then we'd have to take on Russian Communism, another rotten theory, which would be even harder to beat."

A prescient 16-year-old Bill Lair was already beginning to understand what lay ahead for the USA, and himself, at a time when most Americans, and nearly all our politicians, were insisting that we should leave the Europeans to their own wars and retreat to 'Fortress America'. Bill was no 'America Firster', or White Supremacist, or anti-Semite, like aviator Charles Lindberg and other celebrities of the time.

On 3 December 1942 young Bill's off to Ft. Knox, KY for basic training. Says that takes "four or five months" (to March or April 1943). He's not keen on exact dates. Admits that he never kept a diary, but his memory is sharp. He enlisted in the Infantry but somehow gets transferred to Armored. His next stop is 3rd Battalion, 32nd Armored Regiment at Indiantown Gap, PA. They have just returned from Camp Pickett, VA where they had been awaiting shipment to North Africa. General Eisenhower's landing and campaign was going so well that the 32nd wasn't needed. Bill gets his Armored training from a combat ready unit. "Learning from guys who already know their stuff", he remarks. He learns to drive every vehicle in the Armored motor pool and operate every weapon in their arsenal. Says he remained at

Indiantown Gap for "a few months". Ships out from the Port of New York during the "Summer of '43" (July or August?).

Then he gets more detailed. His ship is a British liner vastly overloaded with GI's. It has not been modified to transport troops. He sleeps in the emptied swimming pool until he is forced into worse digs on deck, sheltered by jury-rigged tarps that do little to keep the wind, rain, and ice away. Spends most of his daylight hours standing in line to get two meals a day. His ship is part of a huge convoy that takes a northerly route to England passing just south of Greenland. German U-boats dog them all the way. He sees several of the convoy's ships torpedoed. Fast agile Destroyer Escorts race to the scene to try to sink the subs. The convoy moves on without attempting to come to the aid of the sinking ships. They reach England via the Irish Sea, passing between Ireland and England to shake the German subs. Disembark at Southampton and entrain to the small village of Codford on the Salisbury Plain 12 miles from "The place with the Big Cathedral" he explains. They've been sent to the Plain so they'll have lots of room to maneuver. He says.

Sometime during 1943 Bill goes on leave to London staying in a small hotel run by the Red Cross. Food was strictly rationed. Only meat on hand was Spam. Bombing every night. Whole neighborhoods wiped out. Brits gripe about the bombs and the food but he was impressed by their toughness and determination to survive. "First time in a real big city for me, didn't realize how green I was 'till I got here".

Back on the Salisbury Plain; English winter was cold and damp. They passed it in Watson Huts, small corrugated tin shelters covered with sod and dirt for insulation, but with no heating stoves. They remained at Codford, still drilling, until May of 1944 when they shipped out to the staging area for the Normandy Invasion. Then Bill's real war begins, and once it has begun it doesn't end for another year.

Before he departs by LST he runs through the requirements of his job. He isn't a tanker, he's attached to 3rd Battalion Headquarters Company's Mortar Platoon which is composed of 6-man crews who operate halftracks equipped with a heavy machine gun and an 81mm mortar. The crews are cross trained to handle the jobs of driver, machine gunner, mortar man, and artillery spotter as needed. They've received the basic mechanical training required to do routine maintenance on their machine and make field repairs. Their Mortar Platoon provides support for tanks, along with an Assault Gun Platoon with a 75mm howitzer mounted on a tank chassis, and a Reconnaissance Platoon. They fire smoke shells to shield their tanks with smoke screens, explosive and incendiary shells to knock out anti-tank guns, enemy troops and enemy tanks. They can lob their high-trajectory shells at a rate of up to 30 rounds per minute from behind the cover and shelter of woods or buildings or embankments. Their 81's have a maximum range of 3,000 yards and are extremely accurate in the hands of a well-trained, experienced crew. They are much more dangerous than they look. Bill devotes much attention to the 81. Tells how it can be removed from the halftrack and fired from the ground. How it can be disassembled and backpacked into rugged areas. His mind is flicking back and forth between WWII Europe and his later wars in Southeast Asia where the 81 was just as deadly as it was on the Continent.

His first dip into the English Channel turns out to be a practice run. Second time out he spots C-47's towing gliders full of troops so he knows it's the real thing. They cross the English Channel and stand off the shore of Omaha Beach waiting for the tide to fall so they can disembark. He's bowled over by the extent of the gigantic armada surrounding him. The infantry is already on the beach. Bodies of dead American soldiers who didn't make it to dry land bob about in the water beside them. His reaction? "I wouldn't have wanted to be anywhere else". Later he would muse that "We led a charmed life. None of us killed or wounded all the way across Europe. Lucky we weren't tankers. They must have lost three times the number of tanks they had on their way to the Elbe, and every time they lost a tank somebody got killed, often the whole crew got killed. We were always hiding behind something lobbing our shells. Even when the Germans spotted us, they went after our tanks first. But maybe being very good at what we did also helped us survive. We educated ourselves in a hell of a hurry."

The initial fighting was the scariest they faced during their year of constant combat. Off the beach and into the hedgerows. Mayhem and confusion everywhere. Didn't know where the Germans were, or where their own troops were. Bombed by their own planes who thought them enemy. Got lost in the brushy maze. Didn't know what they were going to run into next. Drew small arms fire from enemy troops hiding in a hedgerow. Blasted back with their heavy machine gun. One of their crew, a German-American from Sheboygan, WI, was fluent in German. He shouted to the shooters to surrender thinking that there were only two or three of them. 35 emerged from the thicket. A whole platoon. They quickly turned their prisoners over to the MP's afraid the Germans might change their minds about surrendering when they saw how few Americans there were. A few hours later Bill saved the life of a fellow crewman who was about to be run over by a German tank. They were relieved when they made it to open country. Had to stop there to wait for fuel to be brought up. Watched the heavy aerial bombardment being laid in just ahead of them (most of the time). Saw many casualties. Especially tankers. Bill said that the 32nd Armored Regiment suffered more casualties than any other unit in WWII. That the American tanks were deathtraps, vastly inferior to the German Panzers. Heard a story from a tanker about a bust up between a German tank and an American Sherman. The Sherman had taken shelter behind a brick building. The German cranked his gun round and fired a shell that went through the building, came out the other side, and went clean through the Sherman. Said we had no tank guns anywhere near that good. That ours were "nothing but peashooters".

Some of the 'best laid plans of mice and men' had been going wrong all around him. Combat Engineer teams that were supposed to blow holes in the treacherous hedgerows to get the tanks through them were killed by German infantry or Panzers before they could place their charges. Tanks jammed up and became sitting ducks. Someone welded at bulldozer blade onto the front of a Sherman and it plowed its own way through. Soon dozens of Shermans were sporting dozer blades. Bill's Mortar Platoon had been trained to position it's halftrack by carefully sighting a spot, marking it with flags, and backing the 'track into it so the 81 could be fired out the back. That worked fine in drill. In battle it was suicidal. Flag men came under fire. Backing the 'track into the right spot was too damn slow. They turned the 81 around so it faced front and rigged a makeshift crosshair on the roof of the cab. Problem solved. No stinking flags and hand signals. But the biggest planning foul-up of all was American bombing. With no ground-to-air or air-to-ground radio communication pilots and bombardiers had to rely on either outdated aerial surveillance reports or their own eyeballs to identify targets. They often got things wrong and kept getting things wrong all the way across France. Meanwhile the tankers and their support units were all equipped with radios and were constantly in touch with each other and with their officers all the way up to battalion commander. It wasn't that the bombers didn't have radios. They just never used those radios to communicate with anyone but each other. Never talked to anyone on the ground. 25 years later they were doing the same thing in the mountains of Laos.

Once they were gassed up and rolling again Bill and his crew advanced quickly making a breakthrough at St. Lo as the Germans fled before them. Then on across France, fighting every day. "So much small arms fire we got to where we almost ignored it." The Veterans Archives interviewer asked him the names of the battles he was in and the towns he passed through. He replied that he was too busy concentrating on the tasks before him to notice. That he remembered the name of a town only when they approached it, then forgot it and concentrated on the next town. Asked what he thought of the French people he said he didn't meet that many. That most were in hiding unsure of what was happening and who was winning. That of those he met some were overjoyed to see Americans, some were wary, and some stared blank-faced in a state of shock. He tried to pick up all the French language he could and had a 'rough and ready' command of it by the time they reached Germany.

Much of what went on was a repetitive blur. They kept on heading east pausing only when they ran out of gas and ammo and rations, or when their halftrack wore out and had to be replaced by a new one. On from France to Belgium passing through Liege. Then into German territory where they found a stretch of Hitler's Siegfried Line unoccupied. "Think we got there before the Krauts did" mused Bill. Spent two days and nights in the dark damp bunkers before pushing on to Stolberg near Aachen in heavy fighting. Battalion low on gas and ammo. Down to just 13 tanks out of its authorized 54. Some supplies and replacement tanks were brought up. Figured they'd stay in Stolberg 'till Spring. Next stop heavily defended Cologne directly across from them on the far side of the Rhine.

But before they could settle in orders came. "Get ready to move out, wait for nothing." Back to Belgium and the Battle of the Bulge. Roaring along over slippery ice-crusted roads in foul weather they reached the north edge of Liege where they began to dig a perimeter defense line when a bunch of good-looking young women came out from a nearby farmhouse, grabbed their entrenching tools, and started digging, ordering them into the house for supper. The girls and their parents were overjoyed to see them. Later they extended their perimeter to the south side of Liege where they greeted Patton's tanks when they rolled in. The skies cleared, American bombers took to the skies, and the siege of Liege was lifted. With the Battle of the Bulge over they returned to Stolberg and prepared for a big tank battle before Cologne. Crossed the Rhine on a pontoon bridge next to the weakened Remagen Bridge and plunged into heavy action the same evening.

Chapter 4: Hitler Doesn't Find a Way

Their rapid advance into Der Vaterland isn't much different than their blitz across France. Everyday fighting. Heavy action all the way, but more German soldiers surrendering now. So many that Bill's starting to pick up their language. "I'm very good at picking up a working knowledge of a language" he declares. Then reports a chat he had with a captured German soldier. They joke around for a while until Bill says, "Looks like you guys are gonna' lose this war". The prisoner's face darkens. "Hitler will find a way!" he snarls. Such encounters don't give him much sympathy for the German people. "When I saw a dead American soldier, it bothered me" he muses "But dead Germans didn't bother me at all." Asked once again by his interviewer to name the battles he participated in he can name only Cologne. The rest of the advance to the Elbe River was one continuous unnamed battle. He arrives there "just about the same time as the Russians". Finds them "not the least bit friendly." In a rare departure from form our quiet soldier makes a brief speech to his little unit:

"We ought to cross this river and keep on going into Germany. I mean into Russia. We're going to have to fight them one of these days, and now we've got the greatest army the world has ever seen!"

Bill's first foray into prophecy. Most of his later prophecies will prove to be true. But many of them will not be well received.

On May 7, 1945 Bill's unit is still on the west bank of the Elbe, gazing across at the glowering Russians. The war is over in Europe, but his war isn't over. The 32nd Armored is slated to head off to the Pacific for the invasion of the home islands of Japan. While their transportation is being arranged, they move around from one commandeered German house to another. Up in the mountains he finds the scenery gorgeous and the accommodations first class. He boards in a large house owned by a friendly talkative lady. Good for improving his German. His crew gets a chance to go to Paris. Transportation paid for by the Red Cross. It would be their first leave of the since before

Normandy. But there's a catch. They have no spending cash. Haven't been paid in three months. Not unusual. The Army's payroll clerks have rarely been able to keep up with their rapid advance. But it's fags to the rescue. Only two of the 6-man crew are smokers, an almost unbelievable statistic for that cancerous time. Bill is among the non-smokers. But all six have religiously drawn their monthly tobacco ration. They have 20 cartons of cigarettes stashed in their halftrack. Their hostess introduces them to the local black marketeer and in no time they're off to Gay Paree.

Once there the other five crewmen devote themselves to wining and womanizing while Bill traces Ernest Hemingway's footsteps. He has read all his books, and many others. Has carried two or three books in his pack ever since he enlisted. Says "I always read a lot. Was majoring in Engineering. Would read any good book I could get my hands on during the war. No comic books!" The only woman in his life so far is his mother. He may be an almost 21-year-old virgin. So poor he couldn't afford a fling or two with one of the many readily available prostitutes in the towns he grew up in, even if he was so inclined. If he goes off to Japan he may never "know" a woman, he may die before he gets a chance at sex. Hiroshima and Nagasaki give him a reprieve. The war with Japan ends while he and his mates are in Paris.

Back from his one fling Bill waits "quite a while" in Germany. He needs more than 82 'points' to rate priority passage home. He has 82. Too bad but he doesn't seem to mind the wait. His "quite a while" turns out to be three months. While he's waiting, President Harry Truman pays a visit. He's impressed:

"Well, you know, one thing that I always remember is that at the end of war when Roosevelt died, right? Roosevelt died. Roosevelt came to Europe. He came to Germany after the war ended, a very short trip, he went back, and he died shortly after that. And then when Truman became president, he came on a visit and I remember very well seeing him, you know, because you gather a big group around, and he made a speech and all that. But, you know, if you looked at Truman, he's not the kind of guy you thought a president should look like. He looked like a seedy little guy who sold dry goods, and that's really what he was. But I believe that in the end he turned out to be one of the best presidents we ever had, because you look at what he did. He stuck his thumb right in the eye of the Russians and said you're not going to take over the world and he sent our troops in to fight them in North Korea. And it wasn't popular. He knew it wasn't popular. He knew it was going to get him into a lot of criticism, but he did it because he thought it was the right thing to do. Then when he left the presidency, he went straight back to his hometown. He lived in the same house. He had the same amount of money. He gained nothing material from his being the President. And to me, I think that makes him one of the best presidents we ever had. He's the first one who really stuck his thumb in the eye of the Russians. I think he was a naturally good man."

Another bit of Bill Lair prophecy. He admired Truman, and his life in some ways tracked Truman's life. He was 'not the kind of guy you thought a superspy should look like'. Like Truman he would make decisions that weren't popular. Decisions that got him a lot of criticism. He knew that would happen, and yet he did those things because he thought they were the right things to do. And when he was done doing those things he went back to where he came from, lived modestly, and never tried to make any money from being perhaps America's most successful spy. No history books. No memoirs. No Ian Fleming Bond-ian spy Novels. No consultancies. Nothing. But I'm getting ahead of myself. You'll find the details of how accurate this prophecy is later in the book. The amazing thing is that Bill Lair knew his own mind perfectly at the age of 21. How many 21-year-olds could say that?

 Finally, he gets a train ticket to Marseilles. Boards a real troopship this time. A comfortable and scenic trip through the Mediterranean and across the mid-Atlantic to Boston. Boston to Texas by train. Then a bus to Waco to see his mother. Officially discharged from the US Army on November 14, 1945 after 2 years 11 months and 11 days active duty. Very active duty.

November 29, 1945. Another date certain in Bill Lair's story. He's in Kyle Stadium watching the Texas A & M Aggies take on their dreaded rival the University of Texas Longhorns. He doesn't mention the score. Probably because the 'Horns beat the Aggies 20-10. He's home now, but he won't stay with his dear mother for long. Soon he'll be on the Campus of Texas A & M at College Station where he enrolls for Second Semester under the GI Bill. He plans to study Petroleum Engineering. Plans to take some Spanish courses so he'll be ready to go on a new adventure to the developing oil fields of South America when he graduates.

The lessons Bill learned from 'his war'.

The only information other than US Army records that I could find regarding Bill Lair's WWII service is from Veteran's Archive Project interviews he gave at age 77 and 86. By then he'd had plenty of time to reflect upon what he'd learned from the war that would prove useful in his future wars as a CIA agent: (1) You can do something really dangerous without getting scared out of your wits. (2) If you understand how to do number 1 you can train people to do their duty when their life is in great danger. (3) Training is of the utmost importance. Nothing can be accomplished in war without realistic hands-on training and plenty of it. (4) Cross-training is vital. You not only have to know your job, you must know every other job in your unit. (5) Small units can move mountains. Bill had an ingrained distaste for big units, big operations and big bureaucracy. Small quick and agile will beat big slow and ponderous any day. (6) Communication is key. Everybody must be able and authorized to talk to everybody else. He contends that a major reason the Germans lost the tank war despite their superior equipment and firepower was that they would only communicate through a hierarchical chain of command. (7) It pays to improvise. If the way you trained to do something doesn't work on the battlefield change it. (8) If you don't know the native language learn it or suffer the consequences. (9) Bombing is a double-edged sword. If it's not coordinated with troops or observers on the ground, it's either useless or dangerous. (10) Know how to get along with people and work with them, no matter who they are or what culture they come from. His Grampa W H taught him that as a child, his military service reinforced it.

Part III: Getting Educated – 1946-51

Chapter 5: The Usual Education First

You might say that 21-year-old Bill Lair had already completed two courses of education by the time he reached the campus of Texas A & M in January 1946. He was a bona fide graduate of the School of Hard Knocks, Magna Cum Laude, and a US Army trained and certified Alumnus of the School of War, WWII Department. After those two 'educations' Aggie-land must have seemed tame to him. He has little to say about his four years as an undergrad. Started out majoring in Petroleum Engineering reasoning that his days growing up in raw, raunchy oil boomtowns and his own experience "pushin' tool" might stand him in good stead. Later switched to Geology because he found it more interesting. Reports taking courses in world history and Spanish. Was glad to have the GI Bill to help him. It was more than enough to cover his frugal needs. No financial concerns for once in his short life. Mother and family just 50 miles away. A happy quiet peaceful interlude in what had been, and would again be, a wild adventurous eventful life. Too old and serious and well-acquainted with harsh reality to join in any of the normal college-boy hijinks. Wasn't a party animal. Doesn't mention any hot dates or old college chums other than a guy who will eventually become his righthand man. But I won't identify him until later. This is, after all, a spy story. Perhaps there were few other than his professors who even knew he was there. He recalls returning to Campus in later years to visit some of them.

Bill graduates from A & M in early June of 1950. On June 25, 1950 the Korean War breaks out. Once again, war threatens to mess up Bill's plans. A combination of Korea and Saudi Arabia this time. He's likely to be recalled to active duty in Korea, many fellow WWII veterans are reactivated. He has studied Spanish to prepare himself for an adventure seeking oil in South

America, but that would-be adventure is torpedoed by the completion of the Trans-Arabian Pipeline and the gush of dirt-cheap oil that has begun to flow through it. The two biggest oil companies in the USA, Texaco and SOCAL, had partnered into a subsidiary christened CalTex in 1936 to seek oil on the Arabian Peninsula. Found some in 1938. By 1943 they had formed ARAMCO to bring their Saudi fields in. The largest pool of oil ever discovered in the world. It was the old familiar boom and bust cycle that had ruled Bill's life before. With the world awash in crude there was no need to hire newly minted Geologists.

Bill's job search is yielding nothing. He can feel Uncle Sam's hot breath on his neck. His hard-earned Geology degree is worthless. He scores just one interview with an oil company. They don't call back. Plus, one fruitless non-oil company interview, and an interview with the Texas Park Service for a Geologist position headquartered right in College Station. He's interested, so are they, but the wheels of state bureaucracy will have to grind for some time before they can make an offer. Does he have the time to wait? His callup notice might arrive in the mail any day. And even if he gets the job Uncle Sam might snatch him anyway. He doesn't want to return to the Army. Thinks that another two or three years there will effectively wreck the career he has studied for. Sees a small notice on the college recruitment office's bulletin board:

"Anybody interested in intelligence work go to room so and so and contact..."

He goes to the room and a lady there sets up an interview for him at a local hotel. He has no idea what he's getting into when he goes to that interview. Not much more of an idea when he's finished with it. The interviewer, who doesn't mention his name, shows no interest whatsoever in Bill's college record. Doesn't even ask him what his major was. Asks a lot of questions about his Army training and experience. Asks him if he has ever heard of the OSS (he hasn't). Asks him if he knows anything about spies or espionage. "Only what I read about in Hemingway's novel "For Whom the Bell Tolls" and some books about guerilla warfare" he replies. Was told that he would be working overseas with Asians in 'unconventional warfare'. The short interview ends with "You'll hear from us". A few days later he does. A phone call from Washington, DC. "You're hired." He wasn't about to turn the job down no matter what it was. It sounded interesting and it exempted him from the Korean War...or did it? The caller told him to report to Washington in late July for training. That gave him just enough time to take his mother on a vacation to Montana.

Chapter 6: A Different Kind of Training

Bill could be excused his ignorance of both the OSS and the organization he had just joined, the CIA. Not many people had heard of either of those outfits in 1950, and even those who had heard of them didn't know much about what they were up to. The Office of Strategic Services (OSS) came into existence in June of 1942 due largely to President Franklin Roosevelt's dissatisfaction with the quality of the foreign intelligence reports he was receiving from the State and War Departments, which were the only arms of the US government authorized to collect foreign intelligence during peacetime. The President had been unhappy with those reports, and with the lack of cooperation between State and War, for years. He appointed an old blue-blooded friend of his, William J. Donovan, a Boston Brahmin lawyer and WWI hero, to draft a plan for a new, stand-alone independent intelligence gathering agency in July of 1941, giving him the title of Coordinator of Information (COI).

Donovan's plan got nowhere initially. Unlike most world powers the United States had never had an independent spying and intelligence gathering agency during peacetime. Didn't think one was needed except during wars. Many didn't think intelligence agencies were needed even then. America was above that sort of shady thing. Spying was something nasty old European nations did. Something akin to witchcraft. Spy organizations were often referred to as "Black Chambers". FDR's own Secretary of War Henry L. Stimson ordered a tiny US Navy Signal Corps unit which was successfully breaking Japanese military and diplomatic codes in a dank DC basement, disbanded when he found out about it, declaring that "Gentlemen do not read other gentlemen's mail!". The Navy didn't shut the unit down. They moved it to Hawaii where Stimson would be less likely to find it. Donovan and FDR were unable to prevail against that kind of sentiment until some of Secretary Stimson's "gentlemen" attacked Pearl Harbor.

By June of 1942 the OSS was in operation gathering intelligence and doing a lot more than had been in Donovan's 1941 plan. Espionage, 'dirty tricks' and secret paramilitary operations had been added to its duties. Despite its many successes during the war the old "no spies during peacetime" attitude reasserted itself as soon as the war ended. The OSS's military and civilian rivals wanted to put it out of business. As did now-President Truman. It was duly abolished in October of 1945, with some of its people and assets being transferred to the State and War Departments. Back to the same old pre-war status quo that FDR had found so unsatisfactory. But with the rise of the Cold War some folks, including its most prominent doubter Harry S Truman, soon concluded that an agency like the OSS was once again needed. Thus, a Central Intelligence Group was created in 1946 to study the matter and the National Security Act of 1947 established the Central Intelligence Agency on September 18, 1947, though it was not fully operational until 1949. The CIA drew most of its earliest recruits from the old OSS, which had been nicknamed the "Oh So Social" for Director Donovan's penchant for recruiting the 'crème de la crème' of the Ivy League and the Social Register. By June of 1950 the 'Old OSS Boys' pool was tapped out and the Agency had come even unto to the wilds of Texas cow colleges in search of promising spies. For once Bill Lair was in the right place at the right time.

When he reported for duty in July of 1950 Bill found the CIA housed in a collection of non-descript buildings, some of them 'temporaries' hastily thrown up during WWII to accommodate overflow from the Pentagon. Its shabby 'Campus' was located a block or so west of the reflecting pool of the Lincoln Memorial. Another Presidential tomb was even nearer at hand. The modest tomb of William Howard Taft. The tomb Washington wags called "the only Presidential Tomb smaller than the man who's buried in it". The Agency's grand rural Virginia Campus at Langley would not be opened for another eleven years. Bill's first two or three months of "CIA Basic" were devoted to tradecraft. "A lot of street work. Following people of interest. Knowing when you're being followed. Shaking off followers. Making dead drops. Coding and decoding messages." His instructors were OSS veterans.

Then it was off to Ft. Benning, GA for paramilitary training and jump school. Regular military instructors, but all CIA trainees. A special unit. Wore fatigues with no markings. Were told before they went not to say anything about who they were or what they were training for. Training cadre was curious. Their most frequent question was "how does a guy get into your outfit?" Hand-to-hand combat, setting ambushes, weapons training. Bill had done most of those things during WWII, so he had no trouble getting through. Jump school was new to him, and tough, but he enjoyed it. Thought it was good for building confidence and a sense of camaraderie, also good for weeding out fellows who weren't going to be able to make the grade in battle.

Back to DC HQ again for the rest of the course. "Lots of stuff on Communism and International Relations". Some of the instructors were experts in their fields. Loads of assigned reading. Talks by OSS veterans and discussion about specific intelligence operations they had handled.

"What it boils down to is you go to a country and work for them. Work on a target. Your bosses in that country will give you the target. They have a list of 'em approved by CIA HQ. It's up to you figure out a way to attack your target. Find someone who has access to the information you need and get them to work for you." Bill summarized.

With the completion of the course Bill will soon get to put what he has learned to use.

CIA Basic concludes without fanfare. Bill mentions no ceremony or celebration. His class of twelve is joined by a mysterious 13th 'student' during its final weeks. That 'student' gives him a brief interview, then assigns him to Bangkok. The "Asians" alluded to by his recruiter will be Thai. He gets a week off. Then is to report to a civilian company called SEA Supply Operations in Miami. The "SEA" stands for Southeast Asia. He spends his week off reading up on anything he can find about Thailand.

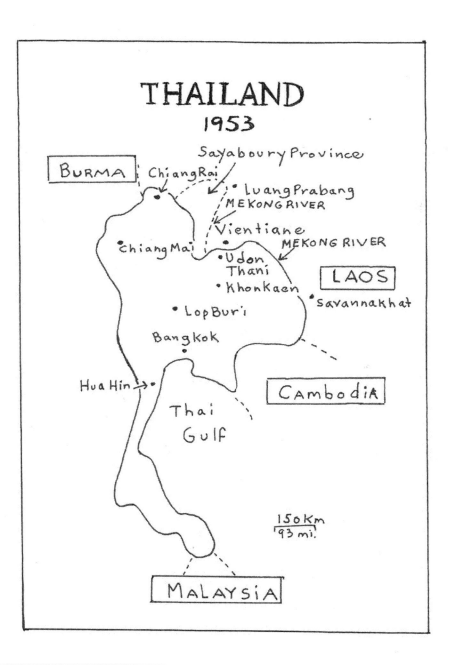

Part IV: Thailand 1951 – 1960

Chapter 7: Bangkok Station

When James William Lair arrived in Bangkok on March 1, 1951 to take his first assignment as a CIA Case Officer he plopped into a cauldron of military and political chaos that had been bubbling for two decades. It all started when a mismatched group of European-educated (mainly in Paris) bourgeoisie left-wing intellectuals and some mid-ranking Royal Thai Army officers who called themselves "the young Turks" after the father of modern Turkey, Kemal Ataturk, combined to overthrow the absolute Monarch of what was then called the Kingdom of Siam in a near-bloodless Revolution in 1932. A thousand years of autocratic but certain royal rule was replaced by uncertainty bordering on anarchy. At the Intellectuals end of the political spectrum a Socialist Republic was proposed. But one of the 'young Turks', Colonel Plaek Phibunsongkram (1897-1964), was a fervent admirer of Mussolini, Hitler and Tojo, as were many of his fellow officers.

Meanwhile the deposed King Prajadhipok fled to his Summer Palace at Hua Hin to await a Royalist counter-revolution, which arrived in 1933. Fought north of Bangkok near Don Muang Airport it pitted the Royal Thai Navy and the Royal Flying Corps against the Army. Not surprisingly the Army won, though not until 4000 or so people had been killed. Years of internal squabbling between military and civilian factions followed with Fascist Colonel Phibun emerging as Prime Minister and de facto Dictator in 1938. The King, already having fled to Switzerland, abdicated. In 1939 the Kingdom of Siam became the Republic of Thailand. In full Mussolini-mode having promoted himself to Field Marshall, Phibun decreed a sweeping "modernization" of all aspects of Thai society. Thai, Bangkok Thai, was to be the only language allowed. All Chinese and other "foreigners" were ordered to take proper Thai names. Citizens of the New Thailand were encouraged to abandon traditional dress in favor of Phibun's idea of Western-style clothing. Vested suits for men and high heels for women. Women were instructed to kiss their husband goodbye when they sent them off to work each day. Listening to traditional Thai music was discouraged. Musicians were rounded up and jailed. Thai soldiers were required to demonstrate that they had 100% Thai blood. The capital of the New Thailand was to be relocated to the jungles of Phetchabun Province in the Northeast. Few of the Field Marshall's "modernizing" delusions were ever realized.

By 1940 he had moved on to delusions of military conquest. With France overrun by the Nazis he embarked on an invasion of French Indochina, namely the Cambodia part of it. A single French cruiser sunk most of the Thai Navy, but his ground troops did somewhat better. Diplomatic intervention by Tokyo in 1941 awarded him a favorable settlement giving Thailand the western third of Cambodia and Sayaboury Province in Laos. On December 8 of that same year Japanese troops came ashore at Songkla in the far south of Thailand to set up a base from which to attack the British in Malaya. Most Thai historians call this an 'invasion', but there was only token resistance. Phibun's Thailand quickly became Japan's only voluntary Asian ally.

Up to this point the United States had had very little contact with, or interest in, Thailand. A bit of Clipper Ship trade during the 19th Century. A few Christian missionaries sent out, who met with little or no success. Great Britain, France, and Japan contended with each other to make Siam their colony, but all of them failed. By 1944 Thailand's dear ally Japan was losing WWII. American submarines had sent their merchant fleet and most of the Imperial Navy to Davy Jones' Locker. American B-25 Mitchell Bombers were pounding the infamous "Death Railway" and Bangkok's rail yards from bases in Northern Burma. On the island of Ceylon (now Sri Lanka) a bunch expatriate Thais and American OSS agents were plotting the overthrow of Phibun's government. Some of them were on their way to Thailand by air in 1945 when internal opposition ousted Phibun and convinced the Japanese to surrender their troops without a fight.

But this remarkable coup didn't bring peace to Thailand. Winston Churchill wanted British troops to occupy it and extract hefty war reparations from it as a defeated Axis power. The US didn't. After a brief occupation by mainly

American troops, the Thais were set free to continue their usual bitter, fractious, and occasionally violent politicking. Phibun was brought to trial as a war criminal but acquitted. There was an election in 1946, but the civilian elected government quickly fell apart. A weak figurehead monarchy was restored, but the new boy king, Ananda Mahidol, was soon found murdered. Just who murdered him is still a deep dark State Secret. A second, somewhat older, King, Bhumibol Adulyadej, was crowned. Phibun made a comeback, this time in a vested suit rather than Field Marshall's regalia. He still had friends in the Army and among right-wing politicians. Not enough friends, however, to prevent attempted countercoups in 1948 and 49.

Bill arrived in Bangkok during a brief pause between coups. Another coup broke out in November of 1951. Called "The Silent Coup" it was engineered by the ruling Junta against itself to get rid of some of its unwanted members. But Thai coups weren't the most important thing that the spies of Bangkok Station had on their minds in 1951. The thing, or rather the country, that most concerned the OSS 'old boys,' some of whom had been in Bangkok since their aborted government overthrow mission of '45, was Chairman Mao's Red China. The CIA was still in its formative stage when the People's Republic of China was proclaimed on October 1, 1949 and so was caught decidedly flat-footed. Nobody knew anything about what was going on in the PRC. The traditional sources of intelligence were blind. No diplomatic relations so State knew nothing. No military contacts except with the defeated Nationalists. No American informants in China, all fled. Couldn't find a way to get any American agents into China. Nothing. The Agency was ordered to try anything, hang the cost. Some of the things they tried at Bangkok Station proved to be less than promising.

Aerial surveillance flights were mounted from a base conveniently left behind by the Japanese in Northeast Thailand. They failed to throw any light on the happenings in China and gave the Agency a new riddle to ponder. Thousands of holes were being dug over a large area between Peking and the Mongolian border. Some thought the holes were for deploying missiles. Years later it was found that they were bomb shelters. Mao was worried about a Soviet invasion at a time when we thought China and Russia were the best of

Communist Comrades. The flights continued for some time yielding questions rather than answers. Attempts were also made to recruit informants from among employees of Non-aligned and Communist Bloc Embassies in Bangkok but yielded nothing of significance.

The Station's grandest and most expensive program was an attempt read China's mail. Or rather to read all the mail going back and forth to China from the tens of thousands of Overseas Chinese who lived in Thailand. A deal was struck with the Thai Post Office to cull out the mountain of correspondence. That was the easy part. Translating the letters from Chinese to English required the real heavy lifting, and bales of cash. An army of translators was needed. Chinese Americans were recruited from the States but that wasn't enough. English-speaking Nationalists who had fled to Taipei were offered not only salaries but US citizenship in return for their labors. By the time Bill showed up in Bangkok this ambitious program had been in operation for more than a year...and had yielded nothing of interest. Doubling down on failure a new wrinkle was added to the mail snooping program. Peking was working on its own spy recruiting plan. The sons of Overseas Chinese in Thailand were being offered free educations at China's most prestigious universities in hopes that some of them would spy for the PRC when they returned home. But some of them didn't return. They stayed in China after they graduated. Bangkok Station launched an effort to make some of those who stayed American spies. Even offered all expenses paid vacations to 'the old country' to their Grandmas and Aunties hoping they could convince them to sign up. So far as Bill knew none of them were convinced.

Chapter 8: First Assignment

Things were informal at Bangkok Station. No briefings for new arrivals on the political situation or Thai culture. Bill already knew a bit about Thailand from an Asian Geography course he'd taken at A & M which "had a good section on Thailand." No formal orientation or introductions. A 'just go out and do it' attitude. He found the Bangkok Office of SEA Supply located in a Thai house and having only a handful employees. They gave him a wad of Thai Baht but no instructions. After spending his first two days in a hotel he was moved to a small guesthouse on the banks of one of Bangkok's many canals. He found 1951 Bangkok to be "a charming place, nothing like it is today." More canals than streets. Little traffic, most of it non-motorized. Best way to get around by "Sam-law" a pedal-powered oversized tricycle with room for a passenger or two and/or some freight in the back. The city was then so small that "you could get anywhere by Sam-law in no more than 30 minutes." Try doing that today.

A week after his arrival he was joined at the guesthouse by Jeff, who turned out to be a fellow Texas A & M grad from an even poorer family than his own who had won a scholarship to their mutual alma mater. Three years younger than Bill he had not served in WWII. They became fast friends and, as it turned out, co-workers. Another week and they were fetched by somebody from SEA Supply to fly up to a remote spot somewhere north of Bangkok in a picturesque valley rimmed by limestone karst mountains. There didn't seem to be any towns nearby. Nothing but a Buddhist Temple named Wat Tam Krabok along with three buildings quickly disappearing into a thicket of bamboo and currently occupied by wild hogs and chickens. Buildings that had housed a small Japanese airbase six years earlier. SEA Supply had a contract with the Thai government to convert that old base into a paramilitary training camp for Thai police. It was technically a Thai Police operation. Bill and a Thai Police Captain were co-commanders. Jeff became his righthand man. A third CIA rookie, Jack Shirley, was sent to them a few months later. No other Americans were involved. No instructions beyond 'go out and do it'. A shoestring budget, but Bill didn't care, this was his kind of gig. When the Thai construction outfit SEA Supply had hired to do the cleanup and repairs didn't show Bill took over. He and Jeff flew back to Bangkok to pick up a suitcase of baht from SEA Supply. Was told he should buy a vehicle to commute back and forth to his new job. Something rugged as there were no paved roads more than 20 miles beyond Bangkok. Finally learned the location of the place he'd be working at. It was 90 miles north of Bangkok, near the historic town of Lopburi.

There wasn't much in the way of vehicles available in 1951 Bangkok. Nothing built in Thailand. Nothing built anywhere else that would serve their purpose other than clapped-out military vehicles, either Japanese or American. Best Bill could find was a worn-out US Army Weapons Carrier. Somewhat larger than a pickup truck. Two removable bench seats. Four-wheel drive. It would have to do. On its first outing it almost didn't do. Broke down in the middle of nowhere on the road, or rather dirt track, to Lopburi. A crowd of country folks gathered round. Several good-looking young women showed up with charcoal braziers and spitted chickens yoked on their shoulders. Had a cheerful party. Jeff managed to get the Carrier going in time to make it to Lopburi just before dark. Dusty and thirsty. Neither speaking so much as a word of Thai, they found what looked like a restaurant, and a bunch of Thai soldiers eating and drinking. One of them spoke some English. A new party began. Good food. Not-so-good booze. Singing, dancing, fractured conversation. Bill and Jeff delivered a duet of *The Aggie War Hymn*. "I think I'm gonna' like it here. These are my kind of people" Bill mused.

Bill hired 30 local workers to put the old base in shape. Soon he and Jeff were set up with all the comforts of jungle life. Mosquito nets, Army folding cots, water tanks supplied with rainwater caught off the roofs. Even rigged up a shower. Jeff was the first to use it. He was a big, heavyset guy with flaming red hair and pink skin covered with freckles. The Thais had never seen anything like him. From then on, he always had an audience when he took a shower. SEA Supply and the OSS guys didn't give Bill any instructions as to what he should do after he got the base in shape. None of them had run a paramilitary training program before, most of them had never been soldiers.

He was on his own. He had no problem with that. He had a better background for running a paramilitary training program than anyone else at Bangkok Station. All he had to do was combine what he'd learned in the Army and the CIA Basic course he'd just completed. Made the program up as he went along. A program that was more geared to intelligence gathering than fighting. To find out where the Chinese were and what they were up to. Concentrated on Thai Police because there were police posts in any good-sized village. The curriculum he roughed out included hand-to-hand combat and some guerrilla tactics borrowed from his CIA Basic, Jump School from Ft. Benning and weapons training (including the 81mm mortar) from his Army days. The best graduates from the first class of 50 trainees became training cadre for later classes. Those later classes included Thai Army, Navy, Air Force and Interior Ministry people. He was impressed by the quality and enthusiasm of the recruits the Thais sent him. Bill had to come up with a name for his training program. He floated "Police Aerial Resupply Unit" past his Thai counterpart. It sounded vaguely misleading like SEA Supply. He wasn't enthusiastic about the name, but he liked its acronym, PARU.

"PAH-Roo...like Kangaroo. It is easy to pronounce in both Thai and English. Sounds good to me."

And so PARU it was. Few people ever figured out what the acronym stood for, but many would come to know what PARU was and what sort of things it did in the years to come.

All went well at PARU until mid-1952. By that time concern over a possible Chinese invasion of Thailand had subsided and some at Bangkok Station thought it was time to end the paramilitary training program. Bill had no idea of who was running the CIA in Bangkok or Washington. Didn't think anyone would listen to a low-ranking rookie like him even if he could figure out who the movers and shakers were. He had been receiving visitors from Bangkok for some time. Most of them old OSS types intent on reliving their youthful days in the field. Boozing. Singing their old Ivy League songs. Swapping yarns around the campfire after a hot spicy meal. They didn't think closing the camp was a good idea. One visitor, who wasn't an old OSS boy, thought there were people in high places who would listen to Bill. He was Colonel Jerry Davis, an ex-Paratrooper Military Attaché at the US Embassy who came up regularly to make some jumps with the Thai Police trainees. He told Bill to write up a detailed description of his program and pitch it to both the Embassy and the CIA. He thought they might go for it. Bill pitched, they seemed to like it, but said he'd have to pitch it to the Thai Police before they'd back it. Told him that he'd have to see Police General Phao Sryanond (1910-1960), the Commanding General of the Thai Police, but that his chances of doing so were slim. Seems there had been some sort of falling out between the General and the Agency and they weren't on his guest list. Dejected he told his troubles to his Thai PARU counterpart the irreplaceable Captain Sinay.

"No problem, Mister Bill. I can get you in to see the General." And he did. Bill expected Sinay would accompany him, but he begged off at the last moment saying: "I can't go in there".

Bill had to go off to Police Headquarters in Bangkok alone, now somewhat aware of the General's fearsome reputation, but game to give it a try anyway. General Phao, who had taken over the post of Police Commander the year before, was reputed to be devious, powerful, dangerous, and extremely greedy. A man with a decidedly shady past. He was said to have connections to the underworld. It was even rumored that he had been involved in the murder of the Boy King Ananda Mahidol. Since he was also considered to be bucking for Dictator it was uncertain which of the rumors were true and which were planted by his political rivals. Perhaps that's why no one else was willing to accompany Bill. The interview went amazingly well. Bill found that he had a talent for writing and delivering briefings. He had picked up a working command of the Thai language, though with a Texas twang. He made his speech in the best Thai manner. Quiet, calm, deferential, speaking slowly, shoulders hunched forward to make himself seem smaller, never making eye contact, never losing his temper. His meekness was not all an act, much of it was the real Bill Lair with the volume dialed down. His natural inclinations, plus what he had learned from observing his Grampa W H, plus what he had learned from observing Thais. Whatever it was it worked.

"That's a good idea. I like it! But I'll have to make you a Thai Police Officer first" declared General Phao. "And we'll have to find you a new base because the Thai Army wants your camp."

Both those problems were easily solved. With the CIA's permission Bill became a Royal Thai Police Captain and he and his co-Captain Sinay went off to look for a new home for their paramilitary training school. Bill called General Phao "a very dynamic guy", which he was, among other less positive things. He later found out that Captain Sinay was the General's nephew. On reflection it must have been a strange meeting. An American acting like a Thai and a Thai acting like an American.

Chapter 9: PARU On the Move

Bill and Sinay began their search for a new paramilitary training camp immediately. Sinay already had a spot in mind. A spot that had rugged mountains, dense jungle, white sand beaches, and a distinguished and important neighbor, H. M. Bhumibol Adulyadej, the King of Thailand. It was his majesty's summer Palace at Hua Hin roughly 100 miles southwest of Bangkok on the Gulf of Thailand. It already had a small camp. A barracks building and five modest houses that were occupied by the Royal Guards when the King was in residence. General Phao promised construction of a second barracks and a headquarters building, but Bill wanted to have a look at the place first. He and Sinay flew over the area in a C-47. Nice stretch of beach but that's not what Bill was interested in. Jungle looked prime, as dense and tangled as any he'd ever seen. Thick jungle and rugged mountains inland near the Burma border. Next to the river that marked that border they flew over a beautiful mountain-ringed valley with a sparkling stream flowing through it. Bill was sold, almost.

He wanted to see it on foot first. He was beginning to get ideas. This was going to be a different kind of paramilitary training camp. A camp to train guerilla and anti-guerilla fighters, not Police and Army observers to man remote outposts. The threat of a Chinese invasion of Thailand had diminished, but another threat remained. The threat of a Communist-backed guerilla insurgency. An insurgency that had already begun in some remote parts of Thailand, especially in the rugged jungles of the North and Northeast-which was better known as Isan-('ee-sahn'). The Chinese were backing some of it. Their Hanoi Vietnamese comrades were backing some of it. Some of it was home grown. It was a small threat now, but it could get bigger, much bigger.

Not long after their overflight Bill and Sinay returned with a platoon of Thai instructors from Lopburi. They plunged into the jungle behind the Royal Guards compound and headed toward the isolated valley they'd spotted from the C-47. It was barely 40 miles as the crow flies, but it took them seven days to reach it. And they wouldn't have reached it at all without the services of a guide who traded with the Karen villagers who lived in the jungle. It was Bill's first real experience in the jungles of Southeast Asia. It wouldn't be his last. He was fascinated by everything he encountered there. The Karen spoke a Sino-Tibetan language and lived in small isolated villages. So isolated that they often didn't speak the same dialect or have the same culture as their fellow Karen. They were semi-nomadic staying for five or six years in a place, then moving on leaving behind the trees and the perennial garden plants they had established. Returning to the same spot in perhaps another fifteen or twenty years.

Bill likened the jungle to the Garden of Eden. Good eating at hand everywhere you looked. Papaya trees and breadfruit trees left behind by the Karen. A cornucopia of wild foods and medicines. Streams teeming with fish. Wild chickens for the trapping. Wildlife like he'd never seen before. Monkeys, tigers, gibbons, several kinds of deer-tiny mouse deer, noisy barking deer. Something called a sambra that was as large as an elk, hornbills, dozens of birds he didn't know the names of. The water was cool and clear and safe to drink, except near the scattered villages. And not just edibles, building materials. Bamboo-a dozen or more varieties of it, rattan, a thick waxy leaf called jaff that made great roofing; you could build a comfortable house in two or three days and feed yourself and your family off the surrounding jungle. He even discovered marijuana, or rather his Thai instructors discovered it. He found them giggling madly around the campfire one evening and asked Sinay what was wrong.

"Ganja. It grows wild here. Quite powerful. The Karen use it for cooking. Smoke some during the rainy season when there's nothing else to do. You'll find it hanging under the eaves of their houses put out to dry there."

"My introduction to the drug world. I'd never heard of Ganja" innocent Bill replied.

His attitude toward the drugs he'd later run across in Thailand and Laos was ambivalent. He never used them but didn't think they were a problem so long as they were part of the culture and weren't commercialized. Marijuana was so common and easy to grow or find wild that it was essentially worthless. Opium was another matter. Some of it was homegrown for personal use or medicine. Ethnic Chinese neighborhoods had small discrete opium dens. But as time went on it became big business. The Thai government outlawed it, then police and army officers took over the trade themselves. Heroin labs began to spring up. 'For export only' claimed those who ran them or profited from the bribes they were paid to allow them to run. But not all of that 'horse' was exported. It became a Thai problem, but not one that anyone in authority was willing to talk about much less do anything about.

Bill's 'wanderings in the wilderness' were beginning to shape the PARU course he would design. It would kick off with a "Hell Week" replicating the punishing hike he'd just made. New recruits would carry only rice, salt, dried pork or fish, and matches into the jungle with them. Once arrived at the mountain valley camp they'd return regularly to the jungle for three or four days at a time learning how to set and avoid ambushes, how to set and avoid bobby-traps, how to surprise an enemy hit hard and fast, then vanish. Learning how to be guerillas so they would not fall prey to them. They would travel light. Work in 3-man teams to stay hidden. Arm light, M-1 rifles and carbines, bazookas with two or three rockets each, grenade launchers. Just like real guerilla fighters. Build their own shelters out of local materials. Do their jump training in the valley once an airstrip had been roughed in. The always-frugal Bill even concocted a cheap and easy way to feed his outfit. He bought six water buffalo and turned them lose in the jungle. Over the years they multiplied to over 200. Buffalo was often on the menu in the valley. Bill found it as tasty as the best Texas beef.

Training was not limited to guerilla warfare. Bill hired an American doctor to give all trainees a basic medical technician course. Sinay found an excellent Thai doctor to join him. Everywhere his PARU paramilitary grads went they would set up a dispensary. "It will help us get along with the local people" said Bill. He was right about that. There were also courses on Communism and Communist tactics, both political and military. Sometimes they brought in experts to do the teaching. Bill had his own ideas about Communism. Thought that if the Communists had embraced religion they would win. That Jesus Christ wasn't that far from being a Communist himself. That they could get a lot of mileage out of saying the meek will inherit the earth even if they didn't intend to let that happen. That the Thai and Lao people would never give up Buddhism. That if they did it would destroy their culture. But then the Communists did want to destroy their culture...a conundrum.

When Bill wasn't running the training course, he was also busy with other projects. He talked to the King about providing security and a jungle refuge for him if the political situation in Thailand ever got even crazier than usual. Doesn't say what HM's reply was, if any. Embarked on a long-running experiment to build a better jungle boot. Collected a variety of styles being used in other countries and tested them. Met a Thai who had studied engineering in the US whose father was in the shoe business. They experimented building jungle boots. Came up with a canvas and rubber model with screened drain holes to let water in and out and keep debris from getting in. Field tested materials to see how long they would last. By the time Bill got involved in Laos (1960) he was satisfied with their design. All the jungle boots he ordered were "Made in Thailand" from then on. Most of the jungle boots the Thai Army ordered were too.

Bill's other experiments included burying weapons wrapped in various kinds of materials to see how well they survived the damp jungle soil; which produced info that would come in handy for guerilla fighters who often cached weapons and ammo for future use. Tested a newly developed radio-controlled parachute for the US Army. A revolutionary wing-like design that could be guided to the ground by radio like a model plane. The radio control was a bit flaky, but it could be made to work. The wing-like 'chute was amazing. Initially used to drop supplies it soon was being used to drop troops. It would eventually all but replace the standard WWII parachute.

But Bill's biggest experiment of all came early on. Having trained his first PARU class he decided that they needed real-world experience and went looking for a place where they could get some. Sinay suggested Chieng Mai where they could operate against Golden Triangle opium traffickers. That didn't seem to be a very promising suggestion at first. For one thing opium wasn't illegal in Thailand at that time. Nor was opium trafficking something that the US was the least bit interested in then. Finally, many Thai generals had a stake in the trade, perhaps including PARU's benefactor General Phao Sryanond. Bill floated Sinay's idea past the General anyhow and he surprisingly agreed to it. Soon Bill, Sinay and two platoons of PARU were off to the high mountains of northern Thailand to fight drug wars.

They stayed at the sah-lah of a Buddhist temple in the city of Chieng Mai for the first two months sleeping on reed mats with the rest of the visitors and tourists and just plain homeless who camped out in the sort of rudimentary thatch-roofed, open sided guesthouse that was a feature of every Thai Buddhist temple large or small. Bill reported that he bedded down within a few yards of a huge reclining Buddha. Loved everything about the temple and the people and the food and the magnificent scenery. The local police were friendly and helpful. They even whipped together a barracks for the PARU crew to spend the remainder of their six-month stay. Their druggie enemy was not far away. Though Bill and his team couldn't see them from the valley floor they could have easily seen their enemies from the high steep mountaintop their base perched on. They could see the entire city of Chieng Mai from their eagle's nest. They were Haw Chinese originally from Yunnan Province, remnants of the defeated Nationalist Chinese 93rd Army Division now become War Lords and Opium Lords. Home base and production center Burma. Retail and wholesale outlet Thailand.

The local Thai Police knew something of their operations, though they had never acted against them fearing that they might anger their own superiors in Bangkok, but there was someone who knew more than they did. A whole family of 'someones', the Young Family. Three generations of Youngs to be precise. Grandma and Grandpa Young who had come to the high mountain border area of Northern Thailand to save souls among the Lahu tribe as

Baptist Missionaries were still alive, well, and at home in Chieng Mai. So was their son and his wife, and their two sons. The Youngs were an American-Thai missionary dynasty. In addition to spreading the word of God they also spied for the USA. Their still operating informant nets provided the only solid intelligence the CIA had about what was going on in the misty mysterious mountains of a wide swatch of territory that stretched across Burma, China, Thailand and Laos.

After the old folks had given Bill a course on Golden Triangle 101, they turned him over to the youngest of the Youngs, Bill (1934-2011). Bill Lair described Bill Young as "a big, strong, handsome, innocent 18-year-old kid". He looked as hunky as a buff blonde California surfer, but he was born in Burma and he and his mother had fled to the mountains near Kunming, China in 1942 leaving his father behind to fight the Japanese. With the war over the family reunited in Chieng Mai. Though he looked every bit an All-American Boy when Bill first met him, he had never set foot in the United States and moved to a Lahu beat. One of the Agency guys who worked with the Young family called Bill "The Nature Boy". He was so at home in the jungle that he could survive, and even flourish, there indefinitely. Spoke Lahu, Thai, Lao fluently plus some Hmong, Chinese and a variety of other dialects. He was easily able to find a spy for Bill Lair right in the enemy's camp. A Hmong who visited the Haw base regularly bringing them eggs, chickens and veggies. He agreed to draw pictures of what he saw there and proved to be an excellent artist.

Soon Bill Lair had everything he needed to launch an attack. The layout of the camp, the guard posts, the number of men, even the weaponry, clearly sketched out. The Haw smugglers were loaded for bear-assault rifles, grenades, heavy machine guns, even mortars. But their firepower ended up doing them no good. A cliff that ran along one side of their base was so steep they thought they didn't need to guard it. They were wrong. Bill and his PARU scaled it in the middle of the night and hit the base at 2 AM scattering its defenders in panic. "We just walked in and they ran like rabbits" he recalled. Thai Police were entitled to a percentage of the value of the opium they busted based on its medicinal value. They netted 40 tons, in addition to several tons of weapons and ammo. Since Bill was a Thai Police Officer he was entitled to a share, but he gave most of his share to Sinay whose own share was insufficient to pay the stiff bride price the parents of his wife-to-be were demanding. He saved out a few thousand baht to buy some mules for yet another of his experiments to see it they would work as transport in the jungle. That experiment flopped. Bill always gave his Thai pay and other rewards away. After the big opium bust went down Bill and Sinay and PARU made other smaller busts before returning to their home base in Hua Hin.

The new Hua Hin-based PARU course won plaudits from both Thais and Americans. For a CIA Agent Bill was becoming a very conspicuous guy, especially in certain circles. PARU graduates soon numbered in the hundreds. They were spread out all over the Kingdom. Bill added a course in radio operation to the curriculum so that they could communicate with each other, their headquarters, and indirectly with the CIA. Got that idea from his WWII mortar platoon days; which led to a problem in need of solving. Written Thai language is a Sanskrit-based nightmare of 44 consonants and 18 vowel combinations. So many letters that Thai typewriters need to use the Shift Key to accommodate all of them. Too many letters and symbols for Morse code so Thai radio operators sent their messages in English even though many of them didn't know much English. Bill decided that this wouldn't do, especially for encrypted messages, so he and Jack Shirley (1927-2003) worked together to devise a phonetic version of Thai that could be written using the English alphabet.

✶✶

Author's Note: I used their phonetic Thai when I was a Thai and Laotian Translator/Interpreter at Ramasun Station near Udorn from 1968-71. It worked just fine. Also worked for Lao. The Lao had been sending their messages in French. The King of Laos, Sri Savang Vathana praised it. Don't know for sure if HM King Bhumibol did, but I bet he did...HM didn't miss much. See *Tales of Ramasun* for details.

■■

PARU trainees became invaluable to the Thai government and a source of valuable intelligence for the Agency. The King took a great interest in the course. Even flew up to the valley camp and spent some time with his troops. Invited Bill and his crew to his palace for informal get-togethers. Things were going fine. Couldn't be better. There was some turnover. Jack Shirley, and Bill's old Aggie friend Jeff (last name unknown), were transferred to Vientiane Station sometime around 1956. Jack became a CIA legend in Laos sometimes working with the wild, drunk, violent, dangerous, and sometimes brilliant Tony Poe (Anthony Alexander Poshepny 1924-2003) who may have been the model for the demented Colonel Walter Kurtz character that Marlon Brando played in *Apocalypse Now*, though both Tony and director Francis Ford Coppola denied it. Jack later retired from the Agency and spent the rest of his life spinning tales of intrigue at a bar in Pattaya, sometimes aided by Tony and other ex-spooks. Jeff quit the Agency in 1960 after his Station Chief objected to his marrying a half-Vietnamese, half-French woman who was the daughter of a French Intelligence Agent. He became an Education Officer with the USAF in Thailand.

Not long after Jack and Jeff left things began to take a turn for the worse.

Chapter 10: PARU Under (Political) Fire

Despite its record of solid accomplishments PARU, and Bill, came under fire between 1956 and 1958; a nasty political crossfire. One source of that fire was Bill's own boss Bangkok Station Chief Robert J. Jantzen. Bill had to be hard pressed before he would say anything bad about another person. Prided himself on being able to work with all sorts, even bad apples and difficult types; and proved it. But Jantzen surely tested his patience. Bill and "Red" (for his flaming red hair) Jantzen (1915-87) were a study in contrasts. Both had served in WWII. Red as a Navy Officer, Bill as an Army a noncom. Red was nine years older than Bill and had already graduated from college when he was discharged in 1946. He became one of the earliest recruits of the new CIA. Sent to the hot spot of Malaya during the Communist guerilla "Emergency" there, which began in 1948 and continued until 1960. He had worked closely with British MI-6 and acquired that agency's aristocratic attitude. Made Singapore Station Chief sometime around 1951 or '52 he was used to working from the top down. Dealing with Princes and Government Ministers and Generals and wealthy businessmen and high society types. He squired Vice-President Richard Nixon around on a 1953 'fact finding' tour.

Bill was the quintessential 'bottom up' guy. Friendly and comfortable with the sort of folks Red would not have touched with a ten-foot pole. His greatest concern was that he be completely accepted by Thais, especially by the ordinary Thais he worked with. He was one of the few Americans who did not work exclusively with Thai officers. Most of his PARU trainees were enlisted men or draftees like he had been in WWII. Their pay was meagre and corrupt paymasters often withheld even that, then acted as loan sharks when they were desperate for money. This was a time-honored tradition in the Royal Thai Police and Army, but Bill would not tolerate it in PARU. Crooked paymasters also had their fingers in other pies like rations and uniforms. He demanded the troops be paid. Created a no-interest loan fund for his men using his own money. They always paid his loans back. The paymaster's loan-sharking days were over. He wasn't pleased but there was nothing he could do about it.

A Thai officer once jokingly told Bill that:

"If we ever become enemies and the US starts a big war, the first guy I'm gonna' kill is you because I'm not sure if these guys would follow me or you. They like you better."

Bill realized that this was not completely a joke...and he took it as a compliment. Even more surprisingly he and PARU's crooked paymaster were "pretty good friends" and stayed in contact with each other after the paymaster retired. Bill stayed in contact with a lot of people, both high and low, both crooked and straight, in Thai society. As his personal network of PARU alumni grew he kept in touch with many of the best and brightest graduates, and some of the underachievers as well. That was not the sort of thing his lordly new boss Red Jantzen would do.

When Red was made Bangkok Station Chief in 1956 the two opposites collided. He brought in a bunch of his own Singapore people determined to clean house. "Thought he was supposed to get rid of everything and start over. Never liked PARU" Bill reported. "An arrogant, egotistical backslapping guy". Not at all Bill's type but he was determined to get along with him and protect PARU. Though he never gave Bill any orders and feigned no interest in what he was doing, he began calling him regularly to ask him for his take on what was happening at the grass roots in Thailand. Getting the 'ground-up' view while he circulated among the movers and shakers of the Bangkok aristocracy to keep up on their latest gossipy 'top-down' view. Eventually Bill found that Red was required to file a detailed monthly report to CIA-HQ of the goings-on in Thailand. Much of that report was gleaned from his 'friendly' chats with Bill passed off as his own 'Old Asia Hand' wisdom. Red never gave Bill a promotion, never even so much as a pat on the back. That would have been enough to piss off a saint. It did anger Bill, but he didn't let that anger get him down.

While Bill was contending with a devil he did know, a devil he didn't know was also plotting to destroy PARU, though PARU wasn't the only thing he was plotting to destroy. General Sarit Thanarat (1908-1963), a nominal supporter of the slithery General/Field Marshall/Dictator/Prime Minister Plaek Phibunsongkram who had been in and out of power for the past 25 years, was thinking about changing sides. Phibun had never been popular with anyone but the Ah-mat (rich and favored ones), and not even all of them. Finding his already narrow support base waning he did what Thai dictators still do today, staged a rigged election and reshuffled his government in March of 1957. Unfortunately (for him) he failed to discard Sarit. What's worse he made him Commander-in-Chief of the Royal Thai Army, the very post that military coup-sters long to hold. It didn't take long for Sarit to stab his boss in the back. By September of '57 Sarit's tanks were rolling in the streets of Bangkok. By then Phibun had so few remaining supporters that the coup was bloodless. Among those who ended up on the losing side of the coup were General Phao Syranond, who was driven into exile, and his nephew, Bill's good friend Sinay, who was stripped of his rank and kicked out of the Thai Police but allowed to remain in the country.

It looked as if PARU was toast, though Bill and his new Co-Commander Pranet Ritruechai didn't know it at the time. All they knew initially was that there was a coup in Bangkok. It would take a while before they knew much more than that. When the tanks rolled out Bill was at PARU HQ across the road from the King's Summer Palace in Hua Hin preparing to go back to the States on leave for the first time in six and a half years. A caller from Bangkok told him he should get up to the jungle training camp and hide out until it could be determined what was going to happen. He didn't take the well-intentioned caller's advice. Cancelled his stateside trip and remained at Hua Hin. If there was going to be trouble, he wanted to be with his PARU men when it came. One of the reasons he liked Hua Hin from the first time he saw it was that it was far enough away from the political maelstrom of Bangkok so that it would not be sucked into it, at least not immediately. That part of its attractiveness now seemed to be working.

Bill Lair was not one to sit around waiting to see what was going to happen as his caller had suggested. He and Pranet huddled and produced a plan. The nearest Thai Army unit was an Infantry Battalion stationed 30 miles north at Phechaburi on the road to Bangkok. One of Pranet's Lieutenants was a friend of one of the Lieutenants there. They had gone to Reserve Cadet School together. Pranet sent him off on a friendly visit. Meanwhile they sent PARU teams both north and south on the road to observe any military movements. True to Lair form the teams were radio-equipped. The PARU Lieutenant returned to report that his buddy said that his Colonel was a good guy and didn't want to do any fighting.

"If they order me to Hua Hin, I'll give you plenty of warning. I don't know any more about the coup than you do." Was the Colonel's reply.

Eventually the Colonel's warning did arrive and not long afterward he, and a Police General who was part of the coup, and two Army Generals who were also part of the coup, arrived. Pranet was there to meet them at the gate of the PARU/King's Guard compound.

"Do you surrender?" demanded the Police General.

"Surrender what?" Pranet replied "We're not fighting anybody. I am a Thai Police Officer just like you are. I take my orders from whoever is the Director General of Police. I have nothing to surrender."

As Bill once remarked "Pranet was a hell of a gutsy guy."

Having absorbed that bit of mid-ranking lip the Police General turned to another subject. He'd heard rumors that PARU had weapons stashed at its jungle camp near the Burma border. Bill told him about his weapons burial testing experiment. The Police General didn't buy Bill's explanation. Insisted he must see the weapons himself. The only way to the camp was on foot.

Pranet generously provided him and his fellow Army Generals (The Royal Thai Army and Police were, and still are, liberally supplied with Generals) with PARU guides. "They'll never make it" he smiled as they marched off. Three days later the coup's top Brass returned. Bug bitten, uniforms torn, hands and faces scratched, desk-bound waistlines noticeably reduced. They never got anywhere near the jungle base. Soon after their return they went back to Bangkok leaving Colonel Paitun, the friendly commander of the Phechaburi Infantry Battalion, and a few of his men, to keep the possibly dangerous rebels of PARU under surveillance. Sometime after that an Army unit from Bangkok came to Hua Hin and hauled away all PARU's weapons and parachutes. Bill was sad to see Colonel Paitun return to his Phechaburi command. They would remain lifelong friends. He would be of great assistance to Bill later in Laos. Yet another addition to Bill's circle of Thai friends.

Though his takeover had been a piece of cake now-Marshall Sarit and his co-conspirators still had some housekeeping to do. The fate of PARU remained uncertain for some time. Yet another election was ginned up in December. It didn't solve anything as there were so many haggling political parties in the new Parliament that they couldn't even form a government...not that that government would have had any real power. Meanwhile now-weaponless PARU shifted to a new sort of program.

"We just went on training without weapons" Bill recalled "practiced hand to hand combat in the mornings. Even took Judo instruction from a Thai-Chinese restauranteur who held a Black Belt."

In the afternoons he marched his men into town where they cleaned streets, disposed of garbage, and spruced-up the grounds of the King's Palace. This decidedly unusual behavior by a Thai military unit did not go un-noticed. A smiling Pranet brought Bill copies of several Bangkok newspapers that carried an article on the strange events in Hua Hin.

"The reporter is a friend of the King. Everybody will think the King has something to do with this. That His Majesty is a secret supporter of PARU."

Bill and Pranet never did find out for sure if HM was their 'secret supporter' but there were subtle signs that he might be. Not long after the flattering articles ran a convoy of Thai Army trucks brought PARUs weapons and parachutes back.

By early 1958 Marshall Sarit had things tidied up. He responded quickly to the drought that had been ravaging Isan for several years. The same drought that helped bring down Phibun's government which had blown it off and done nothing. Sarit had grown up in Isan, son of an Isan commoner mother and a bookish Thai Army officer who never rose above the rank of Major and spent most of his career translating Cambodian literature into Thai. No blue blood on his mother's side and not much on his father's side. A very unusual background for a Thai dictator. His policies during his six-year 'reign' were equally unusual. A Mulligan Stew of Populism, Paternalism, Moralism and anti-Communism. He helped the rural poor, throttled any signs of Democracy, and cracked down on immorality. Outlawed prostitution, opium and "hooliganism". Poured money into Buddhist temple building and education. Strengthened the powers of the King...and, after a slow and uncertain start, supported PARU.

With clear sailing for PARU on the Thai front Bill returned Stateside in early 1958 for home leave and a three-month training course.

Chapter 11: Friends Unknown in High Places

After spending some months with his mother in Waco Bill made his way to CIA HQ, which was still in its shabby DC location. Once there he got the shock of his life. The newly appointed Chief of the Thai Desk and his also newly appointed Assistant Chief informed him that their first order was business was to get rid of PARU. "Too expensive. Not worth the money" they said, or rather they had been told, as both admitted they were so new to their jobs that they knew nothing about PARU, and not much more about Thailand. 'Too expensive?' mused Bill, 'That's odd. PARU's a bare bones operation and most of it is paid for by the Thais'. 'Too expensive?' he'd heard that same refrain before...from his own boss, Red Jantzen. Bill decided that he needed to look for a new job and found out that an old friend he'd met in Thailand, Neil McCafferty, was now Assistant Chief of the Korea Desk. The Korean War was long over but America's commitment to South Korea and interest in North Korea was stronger than ever. Maybe Neil needed some help.

Perhaps Neil did need some help, but his first reaction to Bill's job hunt was:

"Des won't let them close PARU!"

To which Bill replied, "Who's Des?"

Turns out that Des was Desmond Fitzgerald (1910-1967), Chief of the Far East Division of which both the Thai and Korean desks were a part. A high-society blue blooded ex-lawyer who could surely have been an OSS Good Old Boy as he knew its founder "Wild Bill" Donovan personally, but decided to take a very different route. He became a Regular Army 90-day-wonder OCS officer when WWII broke out. Made advisor to the Nationalist Chinese 6th Army in

Burma he saw plenty of combat. Much of it, guerilla-style. Joined CIA after the war. Manila Station Chief. Hot spot troubleshooter in Tibet. Checked things out in revolution-riddled Indonesia and advised that the US not get involved. Took on 'Special Projects' in Japan and Korea. Was a down and dirty Case Officer field man like Bill before his elevation to Far East honcho. Bill didn't know him, but he knew Bill, and he liked everything he knew about Bill, and PARU.

Neil was scheduled to be in a conference that included Des in a few days. Said he'd have a word with him. Bill went off to his training class. Several days later he was called out of that class.

"Des wants to see you, right away" said the secretary.

As soon as he opened the office door "Hey, Bill what's this I hear about you wanting to leave Thailand?"

Bill told of his frigid reception at the Thai desk. Des picked up the phone and gave 'em an earful. "You guys get the hell out there and find the money!" Then "Bill, you go back to Thailand and just keep doin' what you've been doin'."

Bill went back to his course and had some time to think about his two shocking encounters. He decided that the Thai desk new guys had looked on him as a low-ranking flunky who shouldn't even have been in their office. He also had time to gather a few bits of internal CIA 'intelligence' of his own. Like the rumor that Des had no use for Red Jantzen and would like to get rid of him, but that Red had friends in high places. Bill also found out that Des and Allen Dulles, the Assistant Director of Central Intelligence (and later DCI), were old Harvard chums. The same Allen Dulles Bill had taken on a tour of his PARU operation at Hua Hin in 1953. They'd had a good time then. He'd seemed impressed then. He likely still was. Looked like Bill, and PARU, had not one, but two, high-ranking guardian angels at CIA HQ.

There were to be no more Agency threats to PARU when Bill returned to Thailand. Things were relatively quiet in the Kingdom. The Communist insurgency continued to simmer in the jungled spine of mountains that separate Northern Thailand (Chieng Mai) and Isan. Continued to simmer in pockets of Isan itself, most notably the dry stony hill country of Sakorn Nakorn Province where "impoverished Isan's" poorest and most desperate people lived. Marshall Sarit was doing some things to help, enough things to keep the simmering from becoming boiling. Building roads and dams and reservoirs. Sending teachers to villages where all were illiterate. Especially in Isan which had been ignored by Bangkok ever since Siam seized it from the Kingdom of a Million Elephants (Lan Xang- Laos) 120 years before and done nothing for it since. And sending out PARU teams to do what Bill and Pranet and their cadre, both Thai and American, had trained them to do at Hua Hin. Thailand was in a holding pattern. But across the river in Laos things were not going so well. The political pot was coming to a boil there.

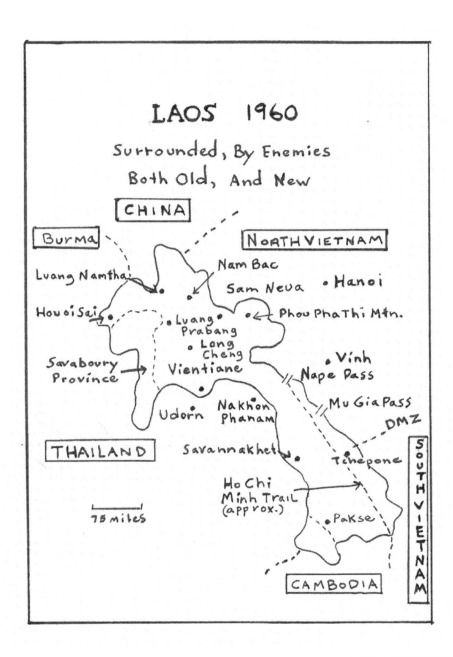

LAOS 1960

Surrounded, By Enemies
Both Old, And New

CHINA

Burma

NORTH VIETNAM

Luang Namtha

Nam Bac

Sam Neva

Hanoi

Houei Sai

Phou Pha Thi Mtn.

Luang Prabang

Long Cheng

Sayaboury Province

Vientiane

Vinh

Nape Pass

Mu Gia Pass

DMZ

Udorn

Nakhon Phanam

THAILAND

Savannakhet

Tchepone

SOUTH VIETNAM

Ho Chi Minh Trail (approx.)

Pakse

75 miles

CAMBODIA

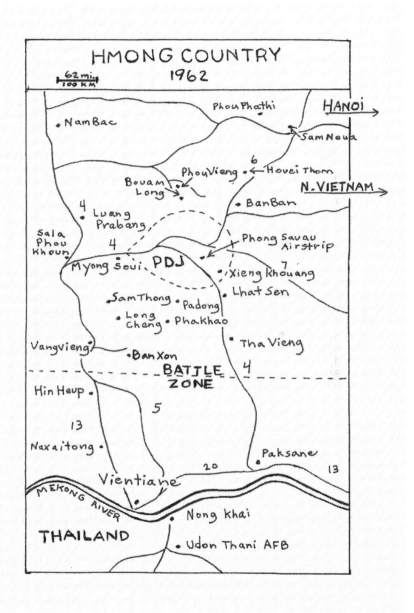

Part V: Our Man in Laos 1960-68

Chapter 12: Things Fall Apart

While the Communist insurgency pot was simmering in Thailand it was a plot, not a pot, that was the overwhelming concern across the Mekong in Laos. A plot that came out of nowhere. On August 9, 1960 that odd enigmatic backward 13th Century Kingdom's shaky, corrupt, ineffectual government evaporated...and it wasn't even the Communists who were to blame. At least nobody thought it was the Communists. Nobody knew what had happened. The Royal Laotian Government (RLG) was there one day and gone the next. Several hundred American Diplomats, Military men and USAID folks who had been busily employed in "Nation Building" suddenly found that they had no nation to build. Bill Lair was sitting in the unused co-pilot's seat of a C-47 that day dropping PARU teams along the border of Thailand. As he chatted with the pilot, he was listening to the BBC World Service shortwave announce a coup in progress in Vientiane and thinking to himself that if there's ever going to be a big operation for PARU this is it as he winged back toward Bangkok.

Though it wasn't officially his business Bill Lair knew quite a lot about Laos. He made it his point to know about it. Had chatted with many of his Thai friends who had spent time there about Laos. Had talked to some of the Frenchmen who occasionally passed through Bangkok about Laos. Had kept in touch with his former agents Jeff and Jack Shirley who'd been there for the last four years. Laos sounded like the kind of place that might benefit from a bit of help from PARU. Maybe not his business now, but it could be someday soon from what he was now hearing.

The very idea that there would ever be a 'big operation' in Laos seemed far-fetched to everyone except Bill Lair in 1960. A comic opera maybe. Or perhaps an All-star Rasslin' Match. One of those "Battle Royals". *Fabulous Frenchy* has already been tossed out over the top rope, but *Comrade Red*

China still skulks in the north corner of the ring his beady eyes flicking about looking for a chance to pounce; while *Baron von Russkie* wanders aimlessly around the ring looking lost, and *Big Sam* America has his mighty arms looped over the east side ropes looking every inch like 540-pound Haystacks Calhoun. And don't forget the mystery man, Rasslin' Fans, small, tough, intense *Ho-Ho Hanoi* who's creeping in from the west while the usual Rasslin' Referee, *Geneva Joe*, flaps his arms in the middle of the ring shouting that he wants a fair, clean fight; and the fans in the stands speculate as to which of the combatants will be the first to get hit over the head with a folding chair. Laos had seen that kind of noisy low bogus drama before but, as in world of Rasslin', most of the blood had been ketchup until now. Geographic isolation had kept Laos clear of the First Indochina War (the French one) but was threatening to suck it into the second one. The one that we'd label our Vietnam War even though it was unlikely to be limited to Vietnam. Poor little Laos was on its way from being *The Land That Time Forgot* to becoming the Belgium of Southeast Asia. That fateful trip began on August 9, 1960.

From the 1890's to 1953 Laos had been a sleepy backwater of le Empire Francaise. A place the French had grabbed mainly to keep the Siamese from grabbing it. Actually, Siam had grabbed much of it already during the 1830's and tacked it on to the Bangkok Kingdom as Isan. They would have been more than happy to grab the rest if they'd thought they could get away with it...and if they'd thought it was worth grabbing. The money-grubbing French found it wasn't worth grabbing despite their best efforts. Laos didn't produce any surplus crops except opium, and even if it had produced surpluses of anything bulkier and less valuable than opium it was so isolated that they could not have been profitably exported. It had no industry. No mineral wealth that anybody yet knew of. There was nothing, save opium, in Laos for capitalist exploiters to exploit.

Its population was at least 90% illiterate. At the time it became independent from France it had no colleges or universities, the equivalent of one high school, one western-trained physician (he was the Minister of Health), an unknown number of citizens-perhaps 3 million, but that was only a wild guess. Roughly half its people were lowland ethnic Lao, the rest were mountain people from 30 or more tribes and ethnic groups most of whom didn't get along with each other or the lowlanders. The 3,000-odd aristocrats who ruled the country and sopped up almost all its limited wealth were trailer trash compared to the much more numerous, and more prosperous, Thai Royals.

The United States had no interest in Laos until it reluctantly picked up the ball after the French dropped it at Dienbienphu in 1953; by 1955 Laos had become a sleepy backwater of the American Empire by default. We did some of the same things the French did at first. Sent out a few diplomats, a few humanitarian aid people (USAID), a few missionaries-not all of them Catholic, and a few spies. Didn't send any troops like the French did, but by 1960 we had roughly 200 American "Military Advisors" in Laos. A low-key effort. The CIA didn't establish a Vientiane Station until 1957. It wasn't the sort of place ambitious spooks wanted to go. VT Station Chiefs served their minimal 2-year stints, got their tickets punched, and moved on to better postings. Most CIA agents did the same. Ditto US Ambassadors and their staffs as well as USAID workers. Military Advisors didn't even stick around for that long. Their standard tour was one year as "sheep-dippers". Regular Army or Marine Officers discharged (on paper) from their units and "hired" by the ludicrously named Program Evaluation Office (P.E.O.) in Vientiane as contractors. "Sheep-dippers" and "double-dippers". The P.E.O. paid them generously, and when they returned to uniform, the military coughed up their back pay and bennies.

This Laotian revolving door produced an American workforce that never learned the difficult Lao language and absorbed little of Lao culture. As was later said of our military effort in Vietnam, 'we never acquired ten years' experience, we got one year's experience ten times'. By the time Bill first set foot on Lao soil in 1960 he had almost ten years' experience in a country not that much different than Laos and he spoke fluent Lao as many of his PARU trainees were from Isan where they spoke what Bangkok Thai call Thai-Lao, but is really 95% Lao. More experience and better language skills than any of the American in-country 'experts' he would meet in Laos.

August 10, 1960 found Bill at the US Embassy in Bangkok trying to sort out what was going on in Laos. He had a lot of company there. Cables were flying back and forth between Bangkok and Vientiane and Washington. Nobody knew what was going on. Not even VT Station. Nobody would have known what to do about what was going on even if they knew what it was. Wild hazy contradictory details of the coup trickled in over the days and weeks that followed though no one knew if they were accurate or not. The instigator of the coup was not one of "the usual suspects". No one had suspected him because almost no one knew who he was. He was a slender five-foot-no-inch half Lao/half Meo. The lowland Lao racial slur 'Meo' was still the standard usage at that time rather than 'Hmong' which is what the mountain tribesmen call themselves. Its use would not be abandoned until years later. Never was abandoned by most ethnic Lao and most Americans stationed in Laos. His name was Kong Le. He was a lowly Captain and Acting Commander of the 2nd Paratroop Battalion of the Royal Laotian Army (RLA). The 100% ethnic Lao Major who commanded that battalion was not around. He was either on sick leave or on vacation in either Thailand or France or somewhere else according to various accounts. The 2nd was an experimental unit trained by the P.E.O. An attempt to create a battalion that would fight; as opposed to the rest of the RLA battalions they had trained who wouldn't. And fight it did, possibly because most of its troops were Hmong rather than Lao.

It had just come back from combat on the Plaine des Jarres (Plain of Jars in English aka PDJ) which was to become Laos' favorite battleground for the next 13 years. Returned battered but unbowed to find that it would not be allowed to enter Vientiane or billeted at the Chinaimo Military Base on the outskirts of the City. Told by RLA General Kouprasith "Fat K" Abhay, the haughty ethnic Lao (and part Chinese) commander of the 5th Military Region of Laos that included Vientiane, to camp out in a malarial swamp well north of town. That the presence of Meo troops in the city would be "destabilizing". It might be noted that lowland Lao racism survived the coming bloody war quite nicely. With Laos near collapse in 1975 Prime Minister Souvanna Phouma refused Hmong General Vang Pao's request to set up a refugee camp for his people on the outskirts of Vientiane for the same reason Kong Le was given a thumbs-down. Understandably pissed KL took matters into his own small hands. Joined by the RLA 1st Paratroop Battalion which was also mostly Hmong he took over the whole city of Vientiane without resistance, including the now-deserted Chinaimo Military Base.

Meanwhile just about anybody who was anybody in Laos was up in the Royal Capital of Luang Prabang (Vientiane was the Administrative Capital-Laos was a country with almost no effective government, but two Capitals) attending the funeral of King Sri Savang Vong (1885-1959) who had died more than ten months earlier but was just now being buried as per the advice of the Court Astrologers. Since the Communist Pathet Lao (PL) had cut Highway 13 to Luang Prabang it could not be reached by land. Since somebody, probably the North Vietnamese Army (NVA), was lobbing mortar shells onto the runway of Luang Prabang Airport it could not be reached by air either. It may have been possible to reach it by boat on the Mekong River though it was rumored that the PL was stopping traffic there too. Not hard to see why some people, including Bill Lair, called Laos Alice's Wonderland.

Weeks went by and still no one in BKK, VT or DC could get a handle on what was happening. As far as anyone knew all of Laos' high and mighty were still trapped in Luang Prabang. VT Station reported that Kong Le's mutineers, who now called themselves Neutralists, were supporting the return of the portly Prince Souvanna Phouma as Prime Minister. SP was the guy the CIA had ousted as Prime Minister a few years before via a rigged election because the Dulles Brothers, John Foster of State and Allen of CIA, considered him 'soft on Communism.' Meanwhile KL's Neutralists appeared to be picking up support. Including the support of some RLA units that were changing sides. The American Embassy in VT was boldly advising "do nothing, wait to see how things develop". They'd had a belly full of General Phoumi Nosavan (1920-85) the tough-talking anti-Communist Military Strongman the CIA had replaced Souvanna Phouma with. They weren't the only ones who were sick of him. A copy of the CIA's background file on Phoumi that I read at Ramasun Station Thailand in 1969 described Phoumi's military leadership abilities as 'couldn't lead a squad down to the corner drugstore to buy a newspaper'. Unfortunately for both Laos and the US his battlefield performance proves that downbeat assessment to be true. On the other hand, Thai Supremo Sarit was a firm backer of Phoumi...because he was one of his relatives.

Still more weeks passed, and some wild plans began to surface. At the State Department in Washington an up-and-coming junior Foreign Service Officer named William Sullivan (1922-2013), who would later become Ambassador to Laos, helped draft a plan to partition Laos into Communist, Neutralist and Royalist Zones ala postwar Berlin. At the Pentagon some Generals were gung-ho to invade Laos, while others were against invasion. At CIA HQ some were backing Phoumi's right-wing Royalists while others supported KL's Neutralists. President Eisenhower refused to take any position. He was tired of such controversies, as well as tired of being President. With no direction from the top it was up to guys at the bottom to do something, if anything was to be done.

On October 19, 1960 word reached Bangkok that General Phoumi had somehow escaped Luang Prabang and had made his way to his home stomping ground of Savannakhet in South Laos. Not only that he was said to have five loyal RLA Battalions there. Perhaps the only RLA Battalions still in existence. On the downside Phoumi's battalions were likely a rather sorry lot and, as they hadn't been paid for months, some of them had already deserted and the rest were on the verge of mutiny. Something had to be done fast. Phoumi was the only game in town so the KL supporters at CIA threw in their lot with the Phoumi-ists. There was loads of cash in one of the CIA's Bangkok banks to pay the troops. They needed someone to take the loot to SVKT. Bill volunteered without batting an eye. He knew that there was no man better than himself to do the job. He spoke the language, had the military chops to evaluate Phoumi's battalions. He'd logged hundreds of hours flying around Thailand in a wide variety of aircraft, though never in a Helio Courier as it was one of Air America's latest acquisitions. Bill was sold on it. He was looking forward to more Helio flights. Even better he had a daring guy named Ron Sutphin (1929-2007) to fly the Helio, a man he'd later jokingly describe as "the best damn pilot we've got available on such short notice." It was short notice this time too.

Chapter 13: Flying by The Seats of Their Pants

The three-hour flight to Savannakhet was made by the seat of Ron Sutphin's pants while he filled Bill's ears with his take on Laos. It was more detailed, interesting, and useful than anything Bill had heard during his last two months at Bangkok Station from guys who were paid to be Southeast Asia experts. Ron had been flying in Laos since 1957. His views on Laos were 'from the ground up' like Bill's. Once they touched down it was Bill's turn to fly by the seat of **his** pants. They had loaded the Helio with roughly six hundred pounds of Lao Kip which at least looked like money though it might currently be worthless. Now was the time to spend it. If Bill could find anyone worth spending it on.

There wasn't any welcoming party when the Helio plopped down inauspiciously on Savannakhet's soccer field. If there was a war anywhere it must have been far away. The scene with its riot of tropical green and spiky dead volcanoes in the background could just as well have been Tahiti as South Laos. Perhaps Paul Gaugin would be there to greet him. Two jeeps putted out. Bill and Ron crammed his money bags into one of them and later delivered them to General Phoumi. He was just supposed to be a messenger boy. Had volunteered for the job before anyone else could raise their hand. Probably none of them wanted to raise their hands for such a menial task. He had no authority to do anything more than deliver the cash. But Bill Lair was always thinking outside the box. He had limited respect for authority and no use for bureaucracy. A classic Texas "get out there and get her done" guy. He launched into a sales pitch for PARU to Phoumi. Five-man teams-one radio operator, one medic, three trainers. One team to each of Phoumi's Battalions. Phoumi had no medics, no radios or operators, and he'd need someone to train his men on all the new weaponry Bill was promising him. The old WWII smoke screener was blowing pure smoke. He had no authority to deliver PARU teams or planeloads of weapons. No authority to do anything except what he'd already done.

"Great, let's do it!" replied Phoumi.

Bill returned to Bangkok and made the same pitch to his boss Red Jantzen and the usual wheels of CIA bureaucracy began indecisively spinning. The brain trust of Bangkok Station kicked Bill's idea around and couldn't reach a consensus. Decided they'd have to consult Thai Dictator Sarit since PARU was involved. Sarit was suspicious of PARU. It had been the project of Police General Phao Sryanond, the guy who he'd had exiled for being a crony of ex-dictator Phibun. Sarit was an Army man, had never liked the Police, was worried that PARU might be plotting against him. Red Jantzen had been currying favor with Sarit so he went to feel him out. Returned saying no go. Then Bill and his PARU co-commander now-Police Colonel Pranet decided to have a crack at him. Sarit showed some interest. After all, the idea would be to help his Lao cousin Phoumi out of a jam. He agreed to let Bill return to SVKT taking Pranet with him, but that they would be accompanied by a delegation four Thai Army Officers headed by a Colonel. That delegation was to tell Phoumi that the Thai Army, not PARU, would be providing the assistance. Things didn't look promising for either Bill or PARU but he and Pranet went along anyway. Phoumi listened to a vague Thai Army pitch and asked how long it would take them to deliver their advisors.

"About 30 days" was their Colonel's reply.

"Too long!" Phoumi shot back "In 30 days the war will be over. How about PARU?"

"We'll have five teams here tomorrow morning" Pranet replied.

That settled it. Even the Thai Army Colonel agreed. PARU it was, which meant that Bill and Pranet were in charge even if Red Jantzen and Marshall Sarit would be less than enthusiastic about it. Sarit would eventually come to drop his dislike of PARU, especially as it confined its subversive activities to Laos. Red Jantzen continued to oppose it, as he backhandedly opposed everything Bill did.

The next day the five PARU teams arrived as promised and were assigned one each to Phoumi's five battalions. Training began the day after that. American

WWII surplus weapons from stores in Okinawa began arriving in early November. Phoumi's re-equipped and retrained Army was ready to step off toward Vientiane on November 21. If Phoumi had opted for the Thai Army's assistance plan, he would have still been awaiting the arrival of his first Thai Army advisor. The 250-mile movement north went well. Bill remained in SVKT to pore over topographic maps and manage a radio net that included Phoumi's five battalions, several advance scouting groups, PARU HQ in Hua Hin, Bangkok Station, Vientiane Station, Air America, and the US Embassy in VT. Phoumi's troops bypassed the Neutralist units they encountered in some of river towns by crossing to the Thai side of the Mekong and re-crossing north of the enemy outposts. There was a skirmish with Kong Le's men at Paksane 90 miles south of VT. From there on in details of what came to be known as "The Battle of Vientiane" are jumbled and contradictory.

Phoumi's forces reached the southern outskirts of Vientiane and began their attack on either December 13 or 14. That attack was **either** a wildly destructive 76-hour artillery duel between Phoumi's 105-mm Howitzers and big guns and mortars crewed by North Vietnamese (NVA) artillerists while ground troops on both sides stayed clear of the city. **Or** three days of WWII-style maneuvering and house to house street fighting supported by artillery. **Or** the gratuitous bombardment by Phoumi of an undefended city.

Destruction was **either** randomly scattered **or** widespread **or** both. Civilian casualties were **either** 300, 500 **or** 600 dead...**or** 'about 700 dead and 1,000 to 1,500 wounded'...**or** 500 dead **and** wounded. Strangely enough the only military casualties reported were 17 Neutralists KIA (killed in action). No reports of RLA casualties, possibly because there were none. The "Battle' ended on either December 15 or 16. Kong Le led his essentially intact forces north to the Plain of Jars some of them via Soviet Turboprop transports, the rest by road. Phoumi's Army didn't pursue them. They were too busy celebrating their great victory.

Soon after the last shot was fired Bill flew up to VT to find the city shrouded in smoke from the many still smoldering fires that had been set off by incendiary rounds, and the streets littered with rubble and dead bodies.

Damage appeared to be random. The US Embassy took a hit and a safe house used by bachelor CIA officers burnt to the ground. An ancient Buddhist Stupa (obelisk) was destroyed. Vientiane is known as The City of Sandalwood but most of it was constructed of less expensive woods, bamboo and rattan. Even parts of the city not hit by incendiary rounds soon caught fire. There were no fire hydrants or organized fire fighters to douse the blazes. Phoumi's undisciplined troops continued to party hardy while VT burned; and uncollected bodies bloated and stank.

Despite PARU's best efforts the RLAs soldierly performance had ranged somewhere between sloppy and non-existent. It was not hard for Bill and Pranet to understand why. It wasn't that almost all Lao soldiers were illiterate, though that was true enough. The Hmong Army Bill would soon champion was even more illiterate than the RLA, but they fought like tigers. You don't have to know how to read a manual to figure out how to shoot an M-1 or set an ambush. Bill had grown up among illiterate, and barely literate, Texans and he knew better than to equate literacy with intelligence. Knew that people with little or no book learning learned by observing. Knew from his experience with country Thais that their powers of observation exceeded those of most educated Americans. No, the Lao were not too dumb to be trainable. That was the old 'White Man's Burden in Asia' crap. Nor were they too cowardly to be soldiers. He'd learned **that** when he was in the Army during WWII. Learned that true heroes were as rare as total cowards. That most soldiers fell between the two extremes. That the thing to do was to learn your job 'till it became second nature and concentrate on it so completely during battle that you tuned out the death and danger around you. Knew that if such concentration could be learned, then it could also be taught, not by books, but by example, by leadership.

Knew that the raw material for an effective army was as much present in Laos as it is in the United States. It was lack of motivation rather than lack of talent that was the bane of the RLA. Laos was a prime example of how not to motivate an army. First there was conscription. Not the gussied-up "Your Friends and Neighbors" conscription of the local Draft Board but the raw press-gang conscription the 18th Century British Royal Navy used to fill its most repulsive jobs. Worse yet the "Corvee" that the French used in Laos and the rest of Indochina to do their dirty work with unpaid slave labor. A system all poor Lao were only too familiar with. Conscription that dragged young Lao men from the villages they'd spent their whole lives in, put them in uniform, treated them like shit, and payed little if anything. An RLA private was paid the equivalent of eight US dollars a month in 1969; if he was paid. Or rather that's what we paid the RLA for each of the soldiers they claimed to have. I translated numerous reports during my days at Ramasun indicating grossly padded payrolls and unpaid soldiers on the verge of mutiny. At one point in 1970 most of the RLA soldiers in the 4th Military Region (HQ Pakse) mutinied and we had to send a C-47 load of cash to pay them the money their officers had pocketed. RLA soldiers rarely had money to send home and the loss of their labor in Laos' subsistence agriculture villages brought hardship and sometimes starvation. RLA privates got no family allowances.

No motivation and no leadership. Most RLA officers either bought their jobs or got them through family connections. The higher the rank the more it cost. The higher the rank the more money you could make from it. And in the highest ranks there were nothing but politicians in uniform and crooks in uniform. Genial, corrupt incompetent Phoumi was both. Concern for the efficiency and well-being of their soldiers was a matter of personal preference. Some RLA Officers did look out for their troops. Some tried to make their commands into combat capable outfits. Most didn't. It wasn't required. A system that rewarded negligence and callousness while penalizing leadership and responsibility.

The training the American P.E.O. provided was unable to change any of this. Most of the American trainers knew, or at least strongly suspected, that the RLA was a joke, but never could figure out why. They were in Laos to train troops and train they did, again and again, sometimes even the same troops who had been trained numerous times before. The American revolving door in Laos continued to revolve. The old Russian peasant proverb "How many times is that guy going to step on the same rake" was true for the P.E.O. even after it later changed its name to JUSMAG (Joint US Military Assistance Group). The training programs wasted dollars by the boatload while producing few positive results. PARU's hasty attempt to make Phoumi's troops into an army had floppped, but there was a training program brewing in Bill Lair's mind that would be cheap and produce amazing results. That program would start up even sooner than he could imagine.

There were two men Bill was anxious to meet as he picked his way through the smoking debris of Vientiane. One was Gordon Jorgenson, CIA's Vientiane Station Chief who he found at his palatial French Chateau. After a lavish dinner he asked "Jorgy" where he might find the other man he wanted to see, a certain Hmong RLA Colonel named Vang Pao. Jorgy wondered why he would want to see VP. Bill told him he'd heard that VP had an army that might fight Communists rather than just talk about fighting them. Meanwhile word arrived that Des Fitzgerald, Bill's now-unmasked guardian angel, was due in town the next morning. The timing couldn't have been better. Des' official title was Chief of the Far East Division of the Directorate for Plans, the dirty tricks branch of the CIA. The charming aristocratic gentleman spook was never far from the scene when something juicy was happening, despite his need to wear skin powder and gloves to protect himself from the tropic sun. He knew full well that Phoumi's raggedy-assed Army would never have even made it to VT without its PARU advisors and Bill's stage managing. Knew that guys like Bill were rare birds even in a CIA that was supposed to be populated with brainy men of action. As rare as T. E. Lawrence ('of Arabia') was in the WWI British Army. As rare as Orde Wingate, the unconventional commando leader Des had worked with in Burma during WWII. Knew that the Thai PARU could become Wingate's Chindits if given a chance. They had already proved themselves in Thailand, and now in Laos, to be not only good at their training job but the best intel gatherers around. And if that wasn't already enough Bill and PARU worked cheap. They brought in their rightist countercoup at under a million dollars, chump change for an organization that spent many times that reading Overseas Chinese mail in Bangkok. Plus, the icing on the cake-no news leaks.

The next morning Des convened a planning session at Vientiane Station HQ near the somewhat damaged US Embassy. He violated standard Agency protocol by inviting Bangkok Station's Bill Lair to attend. Then trashed protocol completely by asking Bill and PARU to stick around in Vientiane and find other work to do. The Agency would pick up the tab while Bill was deciding what that 'other work' would be. It didn't take him long to decide. "Find Vang Pao and go talk with him" had been the on top of his to do list for months. VP had been one of Pranet's students in a Police Training Course he'd taught in Luang Prabang years ago. His best and brightest student. He had nothing but good things to say about him.

Born around 1930 into the small and politically insignificant Vang clan, his father farmed in the Nong Het area near the Vietnam border. A bright, restless, high-spirited youth who showed leadership ability he caught the eyes of two important people early on. One was Touby Ly-Foung, the French-educated political spokesman of the Meo. The other was Touby's friend Chao (Prince) Saykham, the hereditary Governor of Xiengkhouang Province. By the age of 14 Vang Pao was a courier for Free French soldiers hiding from the Japanese in the villages and limestone karst caves around Nong Het. After WWII he joined the national police. The only Meo in his basic training course he was treated poorly by his lowland Lao classmates but finished at the top of his class of 80. By 1950 he was a police sergeant. The highest rank allowed any non-ethnic Lao. Vietnamese Communists were already making trouble in Xiengkhouang Province and VP was the go-to guy when it came to tracking them down and disposing of them with the help of his fellow tribesmen. After he and his crew disposed, quite brutally, of a particularly troublesome Vietnamese Captain and brought in a treasure trove of his papers, his French commander decided that he should be made an officer despite lowland Lao objections. The written exam was in French, of which VP had but a smattering, but the commander stood behind him dictating the answers to the questions and he passed. The Lao National Police was dissolved before Lt. Vang Pao could serve for very long and he was transferred to the Army where he worked under Colonel Roger Trinquier of the SDECE, Service de Documentation Exterieure et du Contre-Espionage, the French equivalent of the CIA.

Chapter 14: Looking for Vang Pao

There was nobody in Laos who had better qualifications for what Bill Lair wanted to do than now-RLA Colonel Vang Pao. But first Bill had to find him. Before he went looking for VP, Bill set up shop in Vientiane. His usual bare bones operation. Rented three houses near Wattay Airport. Lao-style, not French Colonial mansions. No servants. Dined at the neighborhood noodle shop. Two of the houses became barracks, the third a combination headquarters and radio shack. Staff of 28, two Americans-Bill had picked up his former PARU trainer Jack Shirley who was already in Laos, plus Pranet, and five PARU teams. Two days later they were ready to roll.

Bill went off to Jorgy to brief him on his plan to find VP. He gave permission to go, but not to stay overnight. Jorgy was what you might call a 'belt and suspenders' man. Overly cautious. Afraid one of his agents would get captured or killed. Not an unfounded concern, but Bill thought he took it too far. Thought that sometimes you can't get a job done without taking a few risks. This was one of those times.

Five months earlier he had been looking for the militarily clueless General Phoumi and his feckless Lao army. Now he was looking for another, much more promising, military leader and his much more promising Hmong Army. He hadn't expected to be doing either, but then this was Laos. Thailand was peaceful and orderly by comparison. Nobody had any idea where VP was until Ron Sutphin, the pilot who'd flown Bill and his moneybags to Phoumi at Savannakhet, stopped by Bill's new digs for a visit. Ron had been flying his trusty Air America Helio out of Luang Prabang. Had recently taken some of VP's family to the village of Tha Vieng, which had a rough treacherous little Helio strip. Bill went off to the airport looking for wings. Found four recently arrived H-34 Choctaw Helicopters with ex-Marine Air America pilots. Went to the US Embassy to get permission to commandeer one.

Then back to the airport with Pranet and a PARU team in tow. The Pilot was reluctant to go, too late in the day, had never flown in the mountains of Laos, had no maps. Bill promised to sit next to him and guide him. They followed the Mekong downstream for a while, then headed north along one of its tributaries, the Nam Ngiap. Got lost and the chopper pilot was worried. Saw a farmer standing out in his rice paddy. Brought the chopper down. Bill asked him if he knew where VP was. "Somewhere around here" he replied and pointed northwest. Off again. Pilot even more worried now. Found Tha Vieng, a small cluster of rusty tin-roofed buildings nestled in a jungle clearing. Barely enough room to put the chopper down.

"We're runnin' out of time, Pranet. You and your team go looking for VP. I'll return to Vientiane. Radio me if you find him and I'll be back tomorrow. If you don't find him, I'll be back anyway to help you search."

Darkness comes fast in Southeast Asia. The chopper touched at Wattay Airport just as the curtain of night rang down on the city. Cold Tiger Beer restored the rattled ex-Marine pilot.

Not long afterward a call came in from Pranet:

"He's here in Tha Vieng…and he's the man we want. You'll see."

Bill told Pranet to expect him at 0900 hours the next morning. His second flight into the mountains was as peaceful as the first had been harrowing. A calm shining crystal clear morning. Time to take in the gorgeous scenery. A big crowd to greet him when he touched down. Vang Pao out front. Taller than expected, 5 foot 5, almost a giant by Hmong standards. Built like a wrestler. Carried himself with an air of no-nonsense authority. Charisma you could spot at a distance. Pranet was right. He was the man Bill was looking for. He could tell it even before VP opened his mouth. He could see it by the way VP ran his camp. Tightly organized even though his fighters and their families had arrived only days before after a hard and punishing flight through rugged territory from the PDJ and the Communists. Bill had been working the wild places of Thailand for years, but he'd never seen a people so ready to fight as the Hmong, and a man as ready to lead them as Vang Pao. There were none of the usual Asian diplomatic niceties that day. The Hmong were nothing at all like the polite deferential lowland ethnic Lao. More like a bunch of rough independent West Virginia mountaineers. As soon as they sat down Vang Pao made a short speech that set the tone for the proceedings.

"This is our home" he said sweeping his hand toward the hills and continuing around to the Plain of Jars. "We **own** these mountains. I've been in touch with the Communists. They've been around here for years. But my people cannot live with them. Their life is too different from ours. We have only two choices. We fight them, or we leave. There is nothing else we can do. If you give us guns, we will fight them."

"How many men do you have?" asked Bill.

"Ten thousand."

"If the Hmong were armed, would they try to become autonomous, or would they be loyal to the Lao government?"

"I would be loyal to the King of Laos."

"Neither the Lao government nor the US government could support a Hmong independence movement. What do your people want to do?"

"They want to keep their way of life and follow their own leaders. They want to fight the Communists. They will follow me, and I am loyal to the King."

"You said 'We fight them, or we leave'. What happens if you, and we, lose that fight?"

"We move our people to Sayaboury Province on the west side of the Mekong. The 'Thai side' as it is called. If the Communists do not follow, we establish ourselves there. That province has no strategic value to them. There are no resources there that they would want. Its population is small and scattered. Much of it has mountains like we have here. We would be no threat to them there if they leave us alone."

"And if they don't leave you and your people alone?"

"Then we go on to Thailand and join Hmong people who are already there."

Bill was back in Vientiane before sundown. Cautious Jorgy was relieved. He set up a meeting for the next morning. At 10 am Bill was in the same conference room he'd been in a week before. Hard to believe so much had happened in a single week. Only three people this time. Des and Jorgy and

Bill. Jorgy had little to say beyond "Hello". Bill did all the talking based on a transcript he'd made of his conversation with VP.

Des and Jorgy read it through, then re-read it, in ten minutes. Bill began his sales pitch:

"Nobody but the Hmong stand between the Plain of Jars and the Mekong at this point. The RLA is worthless. Pranet and me and PARU tried to lead them from Savannakhet to Vientiane and you know what happened. They can't punch their way out of a wet paper bag. The Commies won't have to fight 'em. They'll scare 'em all the way to Thailand. The Hmong won't be able to go toe-to-toe with NVA regulars either, but they won't run, and they'll make the Commies' lives miserable. They'll ambush 'em and hit-and-run 'em and deny 'em territory. They'll pin down troops that the enemy could be using elsewhere. They won't be able to win us this war in Laos, but they may be able to keep us from losing it. And they may be able to keep the lowland Lao from being sucked into it. They'll also be able to collect intel we don't have now which could help us in the future.

It won't cost that much. The Hmong are ready to fight. Are fighting now with crossbows and black powder rifles and home-made booby traps. How much more damage could they do properly armed? But to be effective, they must remain a guerilla force defending their own turf. They should **not** be led by Americans. They should **not** be trained by Americans. They should **not** be organized to American standards. Send them WWII surplus weapons, give them a few days training by Thai PARU teams, and they'll be ready to go, and ready to kill many more Communist troops. All we need to do is provide the weapons and get them to where they're needed. That's the gap only **we** can fill. Everything else they can do for themselves. Everything else they **must** do for themselves."

Bill delivered his speech Asian style, politely, eyes lowered. Then raised his eyes expecting a response, receiving none he continued.

"No Americans in the field. Old WWII weapons, reliable but hard to trace. Thai PARU teams that blend in easily with the locals. Speak the same language. Are hard to trace. Operation is reversable. Easy in, easy out. A classic approach."

Jorgy continued mute. No response from Des.

"Weakest part of the proposition is the endgame. The North Vietnamese are disciplined and organized. The best soldiers in Asia. If they want **all** of Laos badly enough the Hmong will lose whether we help them or not. In that case an exit strategy should be prepared for them. We must prepare it. Either Sayaboury Province or Thailand. If we are going to help them then we must be ready to come to their aid if they lose their land. If we're not ready to do that then we shouldn't help them at all."

Jorgy and Des continued silent.

Bill went back to his humble HQ depressed, convinced that his plan had been shot down. Convinced that VP had been dismissed as an "exotic", a minor player, not worthy of US attention or support. Not worthy of even the million or so it would cost to finance him and his people while tens millions gushed uselessly into the re-equipping and retraining of the RLA and ended up in the Swiss bank accounts of the Generals and Colonels and Royals. The dusty streets of Vientiane were filling up with smoked-glass-windowed Mercedes Benz's while the Vietnamese Communists were preparing to grab a big chunk of Laos, perhaps all of it.

Next morning Des told Bill he liked the plan. Told him to write up a proposal immediately and send copies of it to Washington and Saigon, which was the next stop on his tour. Bill drafted the closely worded 18-page report in one sitting. Cabled it through regular CIA channels. Decision came back in four days. "Arm and train one thousand men, taking whatever steps necessary. Code name Operation Momentum." Copies of the return cable were addressed to the station chiefs in Bangkok and Vientiane. Bill was to coordinate overall policy with them but would run Momentum on his own with no obligations to either station except to send them a monthly summary of his activities. Operation to be funded directly from CIA HQ Washington through a special account Bill would control. A pipeline directly to a field operation. All bureaucracy bypassed. Something that had been done only in extraordinary situations and for projects cleared at the very highest levels. That meant the Director of Central Intelligence (DCI) had signed off on Momentum.

How extraordinary?

Chapter 15: Girding for Battle

"If Laos is lost to the Free World, in the long run we will lose all of Southeast Asia"

That extraordinary. That's what outgoing President Dwight D. Eisenhower told incoming President John F. Kennedy the day before Kennedy's inauguration. Bill Lair's scruffy Momentum pick-up team was now in the middle of world-shaking action. On that same day, January 19, 1961, Bill was once again looking for Vang Pao. Tha Vieng had been attacked by the NVA the day after he talked to VP. VP and his people were once again on the run. This time Bill didn't have to ask Jorgy for permission to stay overnight. Pranet was once again along. Even Ron Sutphin had no idea where VP was this time. Another H-34 chopper with another ex-Marine pilot who didn't know the mountains flew them into a heavily forested ridge and crashed. They were thrown from the wreck, bruised and bloody, but no serious damage. The pilot was still strapped into his seat. There was a strong smell of high-octane gas. They got the pilot clear. He wasn't used to the thin mountain air. Couldn't pull up in time. Operation Momentum could have been over before it began.

The three of them sat on a hillside licking their wounds. The shock of the crash gradually wore off. They noticed a collection of thatch-roofed huts in the valley below. An old man came sprinting up the hill baggy knee-length pants flapping in the breeze. He turned out to be the Chao-ban, village chief. They were in luck. Hiked down to his Hmong village. Houses made of rough hand-sawed slabs of wood placed vertically with spaces between them. Not built on eight-foot high pilings with neatly fitted lumber like those of the lowlanders. Women and girls doing fancy embroidery instead of weaving like the lowlanders. Chao-ban's house same as the others but bigger. Dirt floor, smoky cooking fire, shafts of light flowing in through the gaps in the walls. There was a table in one corner with a sheet over it. The Chao-ban removed the sheet to reveal an ancient radio, hand cranked, with a microphone. He cranked the generator, shouted "Allo, Allo", then started tapping out a message on a Morse code key. Somehow his message reached Vientiane. VT sent a sent a replacement chopper the next day. Meanwhile the Chao-ban regaled them with stories of his experiences as chief of the old French militia, the Auto Defense de Choc.

The replacement chopper took them to VP's current temporary camp two ridges away. They had been close. No more than five minutes by air, but in this rugged country two days on foot. Bill told VP the US government was ready to back him with arms for up to one thousand men.

"We'll start by arming three one-hundred-man companies and sending Thai PARUs to train them. But you must find us a place with enough of a clearing to air-drop supplies. Remote enough so that the enemy won't be able to see the parachute drops. Otherwise they'll be all over us before we can get the training completed."

"I have just the place, Pha Khao. It's west of Tha Vieng, on the far side of Phou Bia, the tallest and largest mountain in Laos, close to 3000 meters. Enemy troops will never see us there. And even if their spies find us it will take them at least four days to get any troops there."

"Three days then. That will be enough. We'll get a three-day course together."

Bill and Pranet returned to VT to line up weapons drops and brief the PARU teams. Choppered to Pha Khao four days later with three PARU teams. Three hours after they touched ground supply 'chutes began raining down. Like Christmas in January-rifles, bazookas, grenade launchers, machine guns, mortars...and all the ammo to feed them, delivered to their doorstep courtesy of the CIA's airline Air America. Training began as soon as the weaponry arrived. No time to lose. The clock was ticking. The training course a variant of what the PARU had used to train village defense forces in Thailand. Very simple. Day One-how to use the M-1 carbines and rifles. Day Two team weapons-machine guns, bazookas, mortars. Day Three basic tactics-setting ambushes, using wired grenades as booby traps. The Hmong took to it like ducks to water. All of them hunters and trappers and fighters. Figured out how to use the new weapons as soon as they were showed how they worked, sometimes even before the trainers got done showing them. By Day Four the newly armed and trained 300 got to use what they'd just learned. The Pathet Lao, Hanoi's front men in Laos, came calling. VP took charge of his newly equipped army leading it to the periphery of the camp, stationing men behind rocks and trees, rigging trip-wired grenades. The Communist PL were no better at fighting than their rightist RLA opponents. They tripped the wires, blundered into the ambushes and fled in panic leaving their dead sprawled on the battlefield. It was the new-improved Hmong Army's first victory.

"They did it all by themselves with VP leading. No outsiders involved. No PARU. No Americans. Just Hmong. A classic operation. Deniable, reversable, profile so low as to be undetectable. This is going to work! By God it's going to work."

Operation Momentum had its hands full during the next month arming and training the other 700 Hmong for which the Agency had given Bill permission. VP had shifted his base to nearby Padong but Bill didn't want him to use it as a fixed training base. He wanted training and equipping the Hmong Army to be a road show. Next stop was Phou Fao atop one of the highest mountains in Laos north of the PDJ. By February he received permission to equip the full ten thousand Vang Pao had requested. More villages were added to the Momentum Tour. By April the 10,000 had become 12,000. The Hmong had the Communist-held PDJ surrounded. They held all the high ground. The PL and their Viet advisors were in a state of shock. An enemy army had appeared out of nowhere overnight. The PDJ, which had been their home safe home ever since the RLA had all but abandoned it years ago, had suddenly become "Injun Country". First it was just the trails that weren't safe from Hmong ambushers. Then it was the roads as well. Soon nothing beyond the "Red Prince" Souphanouvong's (1913-1995) gritty little Pathet Lao Capital of Sam Neua Town hard on the border of North Vietnam was safe from them.

The Communists didn't know how to retake their lost stomping grounds. Attack the Hmong and they'd run away, then come back and bite you in the ass. With no effective offensive they were constantly playing defense. They couldn't even keep their troops supplied. Bill Lair's Master Plan to keep from losing the Secret War in Laos was working to perfection. Raise permanent hell on the strategically important PDJ. Disrupt the enemy's plans. Cut his supply lines. Handcuff his forces to a zero-sum strategy of having to annually retake the same ground he'd lost the year before. Reduce him from Lord and Master of the PDJ to short-term renter from January to May each year...maybe not even that long. The Hmong would be his new landlord and their rent would be as high as they wanted to make it. The not-so-secret behind what made the turn-around possible was US air support. VP's 'irregulars' got their supplies by air. The Communists had to fight through ambushes, mines, airstrikes...and mud to get their stuff to where it was needed. The Hmong moved their troops by air while the enemy had to slog in overland. But that was just the tactical part of Bill's Master Plan. The 'big picture' was to threaten the enemy's rear, tie up some of his troops, distract him from his main effort of keeping the Ho Chi Minh Trail open and functioning...and doing it all at a bargain price. Not a strategy for victory but a strategy for survival...of the Hmong people and the lowland Lao as well. Bill knew his plan's limitations. Knew it might not work. But as he'd told Des and others it was 'low profile and reversible, easy in and out'. Vang Pao thought pretty much the same thing and said so eloquently at their first meeting. But would he continue to think that way?

With his Hmong grand strategy well in hand Bill had some annoying details to deal with on the American side. Along with DCI's permission to arm and train and supply the Hmong Army came something he didn't want. Des was sending him people he didn't need. Bill despised bureaucracy. Overstaffing went against his way of thinking. He had asked Des for one American accountant to handle the paperwork. He didn't want Americans out in the field leading the effort. But now that word was leaking out of Momentum's success folks wanted to sign on. It was the way things had been done before, but he knew it wouldn't work here. How could he get rid of 'em without pissing off his 'patron saint', Des?

First to arrive was Lloyd "Pat" Landry a fellow Texan from the Gulf Coast. He and Bill had been classmates and friends at A & M. Pat's rough, sarcastic, even nasty, exterior didn't scare Bill. He sent him off to work with the Hmong as Des had intended, but Pat soon realized that the Thai PARU were better at that sort of thing than he was and returned to become Bill's right hand man. Their good cop/bad cop act played just fine. A tireless worker Pat slaved long hours puzzling over the intelligence reports that soon began gushing from the

PARU radio net and VP's newly trained radio operators, and wrestling with logistical details. Perpetually cranky, blunt and foul-mouthed, slapping his ever-present swagger stick to drive home his points, he expected others to work as hard as he did. Bill knew he would be glad to have Pat. He wasn't so sure he wanted the second helper Des sent him. A man who called himself "Tony Poe", born Anthony Alexander Poshepny (1924-2003). Poe was well known in the Agency, for reasons both good and bad. An unfathomable, unpredictable mystery. Plunged into WWII with the 2nd Marine Paratroops at age 18. Highly intelligent he earned a GI Bill degree from San Jose State in his native California after the war. Wanted to join the FBI but went CIA instead. Served all over the map; CIA in Korea, Tibet, Thailand, several other places, and finally washed up at Bill Lair's doorstep in VT. "Washed up" being the operative term. Tough, even sadistic and brutal, yet strangely tender at times. Crude, obnoxious and profane despite his intelligence and education. Skilled at whipping raw young men into effective guerilla warriors. Decorated for bravery, dash, and guts, but also nearly booted out of the Agency. A useful bad boy. But was he still useful? Or was he a hopeless angry drunk now. Functional in the morning. Out of control by evening. Bill didn't like Tony any more than he'd liked his Bangkok boss Red Jantzen, though for wildly different reasons. But could he work with him and tolerate him as he did Red? He crossed his fingers and sent Poe off help build dirt airstrips. They had begun to call them "Lima sites" by now. L for landing anything that could fly. Little Helios to Choppers to C-119 Flying Boxcars from WWII. And If they couldn't land, they'd drop things, men and supplies. Soon there'd be scores of Lima Sites, but now there were no more than a handful. 'That ought to be enough to keep Tony busy and out of trouble' thought Bill hoping for the best.

Des also sent Lair "The Nature Boy" Bill Young. The Agency was in awe of his skills, but he drove his supervisors crazy. Bill knew Young well enough to put up with him; remembered the intel "nuggets" an 18-year-old Bill came up with effortlessly in Chieng Mai. Young came and went as he pleased. Was a notorious womanizer who'd disappear in search of 'tail' for weeks at a time. Often didn't go where he was sent. Bill sent him off to Nam Yu in the justifiably named "Wild Northwest" of Laos, Sayaboury Province, on the 'wrong side' of the Mekong. The triple-quadruple jungled limestone-karstmountained-and-caved home of more than a dozen different tribes, including the Lahu and Hmong and Akha; and ethnic groups, including the Lao, Thai and Thai-speaking Tai Dam. The place VP said he'd take his people to if the Communists prevailed in the rest of Laos. The CIA might not give a damn about what would happen to the Hmong if their "Secret War" was lost but Bill Lair did. Perhaps Young would be able to help him with his own evacuation plan, should one be needed, and he'd likely bring back useful info even if he didn't go where Bill sent him. Nobody had more, and more varied, contacts than "The Nature Boy". He also worked cheap, sometimes didn't care if he got paid or not. Another addition to Bill's pickup team of oddballs.

Still more recruits, both tolerable and unwanted, continued to arrive. Some of them wanted to take over what they derisively labelled Bill's "Meo Alley Operation" and he had to fight them off. Bill's castoffs formed into a Special Forces training team. They donned Viet-Cong black pajamas and Ho Chi Minh sandals comically trying to blend in with the locals despite their regulation buzz-job haircuts. Made their way to VP's HQ to show his 'native troops' how to fight like Americans. The Hmong considered them strange and exotic. VP considered them a meddlesome nuisance. Laos was becoming like the joke some smartasses tell about California that 'the country is on a tilt and everything that isn't nailed down ends up in California'. Everything and everybody that wasn't nailed down in the Agency and the Green Berets and some other outfits seemed to be sliding toward Vientiane.

But the most dangerous threat to Bill and his crew was an outfit that had been in Laos since before Momentum. They called themselves the White Stars and were a spinoff of the P.E.O. which had been around since 1957. While the P.E.O. trained, and retrained, and re-re-trained the conventional forces of the RLA, the White Stars were trying to build the equivalent of a Royal Laotian Special Forces. They trained and organized the RLA 1st and 2nd Paratroop Battalions which were composed of predominantly Hmong troops...and sheep-dipped US Special Forces "Advisors" who were really commanders. A rather lame double deception. The two battalions performed well against the PL on the PDJ despite difficulties in communication between their American commanders who spoke only English and their troops who spoke only either Hmong or Lao. Returned to Vientiane (or at least relatively close to it) in 1960 on R & R. The 2nd Paratroop Battalion showed its fighting spirit by overthrowing the Lao government the US had finagled into place a few years earlier. OOOPS!

The White Stars didn't take kindly to the creation of Momentum. They considered anything paramilitary in Laos to be their exclusive turf. After their initial attempt to run Momentum outta' town they tried to infiltrate it. Sent a couple of their White Star Teams over to lend it a hand. Bill didn't like what he saw of them. First thing they asked him was that he lend them some of his Thai PARU people so they could use them as interpreters. Interpreters, Bill mused, I didn't put these guys through all the hell and specialized training at Hua Hin to be interpreters! There's the fatal flaw in the whole damned White Star program. It's a throwback to the days of the Indian Raj and the French Colonial Native Forces. White men leading 'native' troops to do what the white men wanted them to do. Everything about this outfit is wrong. They're brave and bold and tough, but they're excess baggage. And being big and white and unable to speak any of the native languages they're juicy targets for the enemy.

Having failed in their attempt at a hostile takeover of Momentum the White Stars launched their own copycat version of Momentum in South Laos. It took them ten months to get it up and running; which was nine months longer than it took Bill and his crew. Christened Operation Pincushion it was aimed at raising a special task force to operate against PL and NVA forces on and around the Bolovens Plateau. Lavishly funded and equipped by both the CIA and the US Army it provided lots of work for US sheep-dippers. A grander and more complicated version of Momentum with many moving parts and more than ample bureaucracy it envisioned a coordination of conventional RLA battalions, All-American units like the Green Berets (disguised as natives), Thai mercenaries, and yet-to-be trained native irregulars working together to sweep the Plateau of Communist forces. Pincushion finally hit the ground in January 1962 and went nowhere slowly. All the flaws Bill had detected in White Star soon appeared along with other flaws he hadn't detected. Communication among the various elements of the "Pincushion Task Force" was a veritable Tower of Babble. Not only did Americans mis-communicate with 'natives', the 'natives' drawn from several different mountain tribes mis-communicated with each other-and the Americans. Meanwhile the American Military Branch "tribes" argued among themselves in English while the 'native' paramilitary recruits argued and fought with each other and deserted in droves; and the RLA troops sat on the sidelines doing nothing (as usual). Pathetic Pincushion's multi-ring circus continued until October '62 when the provisions of the Geneva Peace Treaty cancelled its future performances. It's only positive quality as far as Bill was concerned was that it did not play in Hmong country.

While Bill and his Operation Momentum were struggling to escape the deadly embrace of the White Stars in early '61 it was looking like WWIII was going to break out in Laos. At least that's the way it looked in Washington. Marines were talking "Send Us In". In the labyrinth of the Pentagon contingency plans were being discussed. "How many battalions would be needed?" "How can we get them there?" The USAF was pondering how many F-4 Phantoms would be required. Or maybe B-52's would be better. They already had at least one airbase close to the 'war zone' in Udorn Thailand. Conventional or nukes? Decisions, decisions. Meanwhile newly elected President Kennedy was trying to get up to speed. Should he send US or US-proxy forces into **both** Cuba and Laos? How's that gonna' work?

Bill didn't have much time to think about any of that. Couldn't see how Laos would be important enough to start WWIII over. Were all those folks back in the States nuts? Never mind, he had work to do and plenty of it. There were now 12,000 Hmong troops, and their families, scattered all over the rugged mountains of North Laos that needed to be supplied and positioned. A big job but he was confident that he had it covered...with the able assistance of Air America. There was a meeting of Bill's spooks and Air America's flyboys at Momentum HQ every morning. The two outfits were a good fit. Both wild and crazy. Loose and flexible and unflappable. They roughed out what they were going to do for the coming day knowing that it was pointless to plan beyond that. Each new day would provide its own new challenges. Whatever those challenges were, they'd find a way to meet 'em. If 'get out and get her done' wasn't their motto it should have been.

Chapter 16: The Real Fighting Begins

The Hmong Army's first scrap with the PL at Pha Khao had been a confidence builder. A sort of pre-conference season warm-up for tougher games to come. Those games weren't long in arriving. Within two months of its DCI authorization Operation Momentum had 20 five-man Thai PARU teams along with five or six Americans in the field, and a half-dozen Americans at its bare bones Vientiane headquarters. In Hmong-country village defense forces were springing back to life, village head men (Nai Bans) and clan leaders were sending out patrols and ambushing their not-so-friendly PL neighbors. Killing a few of their enemies here and there. Making it hot for them. The PL and Neutralists didn't know what to make of all this new activity and did nothing. The folks in Hanoi, however, took note, and acted. Their A-team, the NVA, was on its way. Bill got word of its coming via "some sort of intercept stuff".

****

Author's note: Bill may not have known where the 'intercept stuff' came from but I do. In 1961 it would have been the 5th Radio Research Unit at Mekhala Station in Bangkok. Later (1966-76) it was the 7th Radio Research Field Station at Ramasun Station ten miles south of the Udorn Airbase. I spent two-and-a-half years as a Laotian translator/interpreter at the 7th. The remnants of Ramasun Station are now a tourist attraction run by the Thai government. They say it was an American Radar Station. Old lies about the "Secret War" are still alive and well in Thailand. "Radar Station" my ass!

****

Around about this same time, on April 17, 1961 to be exact, our aggressive new President's Bay of Pigs invasion kicked off. With its quick and abysmal failure, the venue for a possible, even probable, WWIII shifted from Laos to Cuba and the ardor to "Send in the Marines!" cooled somewhat. Unfortunately, the ardor of the NVA did not cool. Worse yet Vang Pao was altogether too fired up after his string of minor successes against the PL Junior Varsity. He had moved his HQ to Padong and was determined to defend it. Bill Lair tried to discourage him, but he was adamant. Told him not to try to hold anything. Told him to leave if Padong was attacked, leave and go somewhere else. Told him not to build fortresses and try to hold ground. That's playing into the hands of the NVA. That's what they want you to do. VP replied that Padong was a symbol of Hmong resistance. "If we lose Padong we'll lose the war!" he declared. To Bill that sounded like "a lot of Washington crap". He was 'going native', thinking like a Hmong while VP was 'going American'. The split between the two of them would only get worse as time went on.

Still Bill was determined to let VP make his own decisions even if those decisions brought disaster. It was going to be a long war. Might as well learn your necessary lessons up front. It was his army and his people. The US was just providing him with supplies. Word of the Bay of Pigs disaster reached Padong on April 18. The three Agency men there, one of them Bill Young, were flabbergasted. VP was mad. How could the 'great and powerful OZ' USA fail to carry off the invasion of a little two-bit island like Cuba? "The Nature Boy" and his comrades didn't have an answer, they were as dumbfounded as he was. Even the arrival of a planeload of Green Berets in uniform, not black pajamas, failed to reassure him. To all assembled except VP the coming battle looked like an unequal contest. The very kind of battle the Hmong should **not** be fighting.

Already having taken control of much of the PDJ the enemy pushed off the south side of it toward Padong. It was a large and varied force. NVA regulars-infantry and artillery, PL/NVA 'mixed battalions'-Lao troops with Vietnamese officers and 'stiffeners' to make them fight, PL 'regulars' to do their usual bit as front men. Bill Young thought he even heard Chinese crackling over the air waves. Padong was at the edge of open country separated from it by a single low ridge which the enemy began to attack. VP's troops held the ridge for two days with the help US Green Beret mortar support, including a 4.2-inch mortar fired from a helicopter. Initially frustrated the enemy began to hurl in its own artillery fire which proved so heavy and accurate that VP decided to let his noncombatants evacuate. They headed for his old base of Pha Khao a two-day hike away. On May 3, 1961 US Ambassador-without-portfolio Averell Harriman announced that a cease-fire had been negotiated in all of Laos. That paper 'cease fire' had no effect at Padong. NVA artillerists began to lambaste Padong with US 75mm Pack Howitzers and heavier 105's that had been captured from the RLA which chased everyone into the trenches. Bill's CIA contingent consisted of Bill Young, Jack Shirley and Tony Poe. Bill and Jack hated each other's guts. Tony was always an accident waiting to happen. Not exactly the Dream Team. Bill would have preferred not to have them there at all, but then he would have also preferred not to have VP's Army, and its dependents, and all the wildly assorted US military types there as well.

On May 13 while the NVA continued to probe the defenses of Padong, they also attacked a Hmong and PARU mountaintop (7300 feet) outpost at Muong Ngat 80 miles to the east of it in the shadow of the North Vietnam border. They came on in human waves and died by hundreds as defenders plied their heavy machine guns in overlapping fields of fire down onto them. Heedless of casualties the waves continued until the enemy reached the summit and slaughtered both its defenders and resident civilians. News of the tragedy shook morale when it reached Padong. The fact that Muong Ngat was VP's birthplace did not escape attention. Muong Ngat was of little strategic importance. This was clearly revenge killing on a large scale. Payback for the Hmong resurgence. This was the kind of war VP was spoiling for whether he knew it or not. On May 15 the enemy began to ramp up its attack on Padong following a pattern that would become all too familiar in future battles. Now the NVA human waves hit the ridge the Hmong had successfully defended earlier and carried it with heavy losses; set up their big guns behind that ridge where the US 4.2-inch mortars couldn't hit them. Started to pound away. Their patrols became larger and more aggressive. Their bombardments heavier. Amidst the noise and chaos Jack Shirley sat quietly under a tree sipping a beer and reading a newspaper both of which had just been delivered by chopper. The same chopper had also delivered a Colonel who was looking for one of his White Star Teams. He asked Jack where he could find them.

"Over there, hiding in that bunker" he replied. Score one for Team Momentum.

Bill Lair always admired Jack's coolness under fire. The mixed collection of American fighters present at Padong were very effective, but only because Jack Shirley, who never fired a shot, was there to lead their leaders and keep them out of trouble. Danger brought out the best in him. When there was no danger, he was lackadaisical, lazy and had to be pointed in the right direction. Still even then he was always pleasant and humorous company.

While Jack caught up on the news of the outside world, the NVA continued to grind down the defenders of Padong methodically, taking their time at it, in no hurry. Clouds of slash-and-burn smoke from the smoldering rice stubble on the surrounding hillsides was limiting visibility. Soon the first rains of the monsoon would blot it out completely. Morale was on the verge of collapse. Bill Young did his disappearing act. A Green Beret panicked under the continual bombardment and went AWOL. Later returned and was airlifted out.

On May 31 an Air America H-34 chopper got lost in the smoke and crashed into a nearby mountainside killing all on board. Hmong soldiers began to trickle away. Several Americans were captured by the enemy. As what proved to be Padong's final implosion continued Jack Shirley was zipping around by chopper visiting Hmong outposts to check on them and gather intel. When he returned to Padong he found a shaken-looking VP wanting to get out and mentioning something about going to a nearby airstrip to get some rice. Jack told the chopper pilot to take him where he wanted to go and not bring him back. That Padong was "closed for business" for the rest of the day. Minutes later Jack was handed a message from Pat Landry in VT "NVA to attack the following coordinates at 1600 HRS". It was 1550 HRS and he was standing on top of those coordinates. Jack and Tony, the remaining US Special Forces, the Thai PARU, and what was left of Padong's Hmong defenders (roughly four or five hundred by this time) moved out taking with them what they could carry, including their wounded, and destroying the rest. They made their exit under a hail of small arms fire coolly and without panic. As soon as it got dark the Hmong split into small groups as was their practice. Some turned on flashlights and drew heavy NVA artillery fire. Some were picked up by H-34 choppers and taken to Pha Khao. The rest walked. June 6, 1961 was the official end of the Battle of Padong.

A wounded Tony Poe hoofed it out carrying a young child with him. Even in the heat of battle he remained as ever both tender and vicious. Hmong losses ~d been relatively light, certainly light compared to the enemy's losses. But, ~icans would soon begin to learn in South Vietnam, body-counts don't mean shit. The enemy had won the day and demoralized the friendlies. They had taught **their** enemies a lesson they would not forget. They didn't hang around after the fight. The monsoon rains would soon arrive, and they needed to shorten their supply lines. Four days after the Hmong retreat VP's scouts returned to Padong and found it deserted. Vang Pao had blown it. His manic-depressive nature plunged him into despair. It took him a long time to bounce back, but he didn't learn Bill's lesson. By the time he recovered he was at Long Cheng which would become the ultimate base that he and his people "could not afford to lose". The American armchair strategists in Washington were as bummed out a VP was.

Bill had seen it all coming but wasn't about to gloat over his wisdom. The battle that "couldn't be lost" was lost, but not the war. Other than making Padong **their** symbol the Communists accomplished nothing of lasting value and paid a high price for it. They left, the rains came, and when dry weather returned, they found themselves in the same fix they'd been in before they attacked Padong. The annual see-saw battle over the PDJ had commenced. It would be years before it would end.

Chapter 17: Mister Pop's War

While Bill Lair was fuming over VP's pigheaded refusal to abandon his Padong HQ there was another American in Laos who was also trying to save the Hmong from self-inflicted disaster. A man whose experiences in Laos seemed to be tracking his own. His name was Edgar Buell (1913-1981); "Mister Pop" to the many people, mostly Hmong, who came to know and love him. An evil drug-dealing capitalist stooge war criminal and CIA master spy to those, mostly from the American lunatic left, who didn't. Pop arrived in VT in June 1960 as an agricultural advisor with International Voluntary Services (IVS), a sort of civilian Peace Corps with a religious bent. At $75 a month he was making an inauspicious start as a capitalist stooge. Assigned to a mission at Lhat Houang, a small half-Hmong, half-Lao town in the foothills just off the southwest corner of the PDJ, to be part of a USAID-financed Agricultural Training School. His fellow volunteers were freshly minted college grads in their early 20's none of whom had any agricultural background. He was twice their age, had never been anywhere near a college or university, and possessed more ag knowledge and experience that any of them were likely to acquire in their lifetimes. Upon touring their half-finished Ag Academy his heart sank. The school, which had been planned by a couple of non-farmers with Ivy League degrees who spent most of their time at USAID HQ in VT, was a disaster in the making. A small fleet of trucks and tractors and assorted equipment...even a bulldozer...sat rusting in the tropic heat and humidity. The master plan was to establish a 500-acre model Iowa corn farm in the wilds of southeast Asia on a stretch of exhausted worked-out land that Pop knew would not produce so much as a single bushel of corn.

If that wasn't already bad enough his new boss was a bigoted middle-aged Bible-thumper whose sole interest was saving savage souls. Pop considered himself a good Christian, though far from a pious one. He attended church regularly, did his bit as a member of his congregation. Had decided to join IVS after his wife died when a missionary gave a talk about it at his church. Pop, like Bill Lair, wasn't a guy to sit around moping. His young fellow volunteers had the moping franchise covered. Within a month he had essentially taken charge of the operation at Lhat Houang leaving his boss to preach to the few 'natives' who showed up for his services and hymn singing out of curiosity. He led his young crew and some of the local Lao and Hmong in completing the Ag School construction project...which had been in the works for three years...in two months. He knew that it probably never would be used but IVS had a contract with USAID to build it. While that construction project was underway word reached Lhat Houang, on August 16, a week after the fact, of Kong Le's coup. Nobody knew what was going on, not even the American P.E.O. Colonel advising the French/Lao outpost at nearby Khang Khay Base on the PDJ. They still didn't know what was happening on September 15 when construction was officially completed. By then Pop had made some friends among the Hmong, including a man who turned out to be one of Vang Pao's most trusted lieutenants...and heir apparent through his clan to a chunk of the PDJ and environs opium trade. On September 26 Pop's new friend led him off on a one-week tour of his clan's territory which included a tiger hunt and a visit to the Million Elephants (Lan Xang) Bar in Xienghouangville, which was the capital of Xiengkhouang Province and the home base of the Corsican Mafia's X-to-Saigon-to-Marseilles opium-to-paste-to-heroin drug trade.

Pop returned to Lhat Houang better educated, and decided to pitch into another project as there was still no word of what was going on in VT. Since Pop's Bible-belting boss had bugged out without notice or explanation while he was on tour, he was no longer around to annoy both the IVS volunteers and the locals. As usual the USAID guys were absent, so he dug in their files and found a project that had been gathering dust there for years. The project for which they had acquired the dozer. A dam to be built at the nearby town of Lhat Sen to provide drinking and irrigation water. Nothing had been done on it so far. Pop called his Ag School construction team together and pitched them the project at roughly the same time Bill was pitching his PARU project to General Phoumi a few hundred miles away. Phoumi bought Bill's project, but Pop's crew didn't buy his. They had a higher priority, repairing Route 4 to Paksane, which had been closed for two years. It was their only link to VT. Nothing in the USAID files for that project but Pop didn't care. Road building first, **then** dam building. They had all the supplies they needed, including a file cabinet full of Lao Kip. A convoy headed by the Big Cat ground its way slowly south grading the road and rebuilding washed out bridges as it went. By the end of September, the roadwork was complete, and the dam building commenced. By November 30 that was done too.

Pop had been getting a bit of well-deserved rest in Lhat Houang on December 12, 1960 when he received an unexpected visitor. The opium-lord-in-waiting friend who'd led his earlier PDJ Tour brought a certain Colonel Vang Pao to see him. The two of them got right to the point. The Communists-PL and NVA; and Kong Le's Neutralists backed by Soviet advisors and aircraft, were about to take over the PDJ and Vang Pao and his people were pulling out. Many were already gone. VP had plans for them. They would move off to a string of seven mountaintop fortress villages surrounding the PDJ and operate against the Communists from there. But they'd have big problems when they got where they were going. They'd have to abandon their crops. Would have only what food they could carry with them. Had only cross-bows and black powder muskets to defend themselves. They'd need help to survive, and they'd need it fast. VP estimated that there were 120,000 of them and they had enough supplies to last 3-4 months. After that, starvation.

"Why do you think I can help you?" gasped Pop. "I'm a 75-buck-month nothing."

"A nothing who completed an Ag School building, repaired a washed-out stretch of road, and built a dam in five months? That's the kind of 'nothing' we need."

Pop promised he'd do what he could, though he had no idea what that would be. VP swore him to secrecy, even from his fellow Americans if need be, and showed him his plans. Where he was sending his people, what they would need once they got there, how many of them there would be at each spot. He admitted that the 'how many' part was nothing but a wild guess. Nobody had ever known how many Hmong there were, not even the Hmong themselves.

Three weeks later Bill would have his own meeting with VP at Tha Vieng. It would be a while before he'd meet his doppelganger Pop Buell. Between the two of them they'd find a way to keep the Hmong people alive until they could establish their new villages and arm themselves to resist their enemies. The task of arming and training the Hmong didn't faze Bill. The seemingly impossible task of feeding 120,000 Hmong didn't faze Pop. The two of them looked about as far from being cinematic heroes as two humans could be. Bill the un-Texas-ly quiet, diffident, "Asian". Pop the small shriveled (5-7 and around 130) hunk of ungrammatical Ohio beef jerky. Both men infinitely tougher, and smarter, than they looked.

Pop had told VP he'd do everything he could to help the Hmong on December 12, 1960, but he wasn't able to make a fast start of it because he was stuck on the PDJ. No flights in or out. He thought of trying to walk out but with Communists swarming everywhere decided that might not be a good idea. He hung around with the P.E.O. Colonel, some leftover "Soldiers of France", and a, probably useless, RLA Battalion at Khang Khay Base. Evacuation flights were promised but failed to materialize. A Thai Paratroop Battalion was expected but didn't show. Finally, one of Kong Le's now-Soviet backed Neutralist Battalions did show and began to bombard Phonsavane Airport at the same time a Thai Army C-46 came in. Pop, the Colonel, and some others scrambled aboard as the firing stopped. Pop thought the halt must be a humanitarian gesture. He later met up with Kong Le after he switched to the non-Communist side and was told it wasn't; that the Neuts had just run out of ammo. The old Dakota took Pop to Bangkok where he was once again stranded, though much more safely and comfortably this time. On March 14, 1961 Americans were banned from Laos as per decree of the new US President, JFK. Pop cooled his heels in BKK for a while, then lost patience with Young Jack and returned to Vientiane despite his decree. There, on March 26, 1961, he found Bill Lair and his crew and a bunch of Air America flyboys who were also ignoring their Commander-in-Chief's orders.

The two of them exchanged information. Pop was surprised to find out that much of the work he had discussed with VP in December was already being done, or at least started, but much more needed doing. The Lao, and Isan

Thai, rule for survival calls for one mun (as in 'moon') of rice per month for each adult and half that for each child. A mun is 12 kilograms (26.4 pounds). Rough it out to one pound of sticky (glutinous) rice per day in English per adult and a half-pound per child. 45 tons of rice a day to feed 120,000 people some of whom were already starving. That was a lot more than Bill's Air America flyboys were delivering at present. And even that wouldn't be enough. VP's estimated 120,000 were already there, but still more were coming in. His seven camps were overcrowded. He had to set up more camps and Air America would need to bring in far more than 45 tons a day to build up stocks to get his people through the monsoon season when there would be little safe flying weather. A season that was no more than three months away.

The rice situation looked grim on March 26, but five days later JFK lifted his 'No Americans in Laos' ban. Soon Air America was winging in 60 tons per day. When USAID returned, its country chief lent Bill and Pop 28 of his people for six months. Soon most of them were in the wild mountains ringing the PDJ distributing rice and meds and pots and pans. "Soft rice" as the Air America boys called it, as opposed to "hard rice" guns and ammo. The Hmong didn't need "hard rice" yet, they needed to survive so they could keep fighting. Or maybe they wouldn't need to fight after all. On May 16 a ceasefire in Laos was declared. The NVA ignored it and continued to attack Padong even though their government in Hanoi had agreed to it. As they insisted that they had no troops in Laos they were therefor abiding by the ceasefire. After having driven VP's army from Padong they did observe the ceasefire for the next three months until the monsoon was over. Then they started violating it again. All Americans were on the same page in Laos for the next six months. It was the first time that had ever happened. Unfortunately, it would never happen again after that. Some of the Hmong starved to death, how many nobody knows. The problem was too big for even the best efforts of all involved. Meanwhile the elusive "Nature Boy" Bill Young returned from the bush to report that he'd found the perfect place for a big refugee camp near a tiny Hmong village called Long Cheng (Long Tieng on French maps) 75 miles ⁻ᵗ of VP's Pha Khao HQ. It had everything needed. It was far enough from ⁻ be safe from the fighting. Had good water, decent soil and room for gardens; and most importantly it had a flat easily cleared stretch of ground long enough to land and take off a C-123 transport. Only one small flaw. There was a steep ridge behind it that, if taken by an enemy, would make it a sitting duck. By October of '61 a refugee camp was being established at Long Cheng under the direction of Pop Buell and financed by USAID. By early-1962 a runway had been built and it had become Vang Pao's HQ.

The period between the monsoons of 1961 (June-August) and the monsoons of 1962 was a relatively peaceful one in Laos. A few PL and NVA snuck out onto the PDJ and were mostly left alone by the Hmong. VP, now relocated to Long Cheng, regained his composure and didn't feel the need to engage in more "symbolic" battles. As Bill had predicted, the Padong "debacle" was quickly forgotten and replaced with a new disaster-in-the-making in the far north of Laos near the China border. More of General Phoumi's handiwork. Much worse results than his "Battle of Vientiane" this time. The small isolated town of Luang Namtha, population about 2,000, was the sole remaining outpost of the Royal Lao Government (RLG) in a remote mountainous sparsely populated area of far northern Laos in January 1962 when Phoumi started sending RLA troops there. Eventually he had nearly one fourth of the RLA (5,000 troops) in the ridge-rimmed valley that strongly resembled Dienbienphu. Even the P.E.O. and US Special Forces thought his plan was crazy, though they sent him advisors anyway. Luang Namtha was just 15 miles from the China border. On May 8, 1962 a combined NVA and Chinese Red Army force overran it and sent its Lao defenders fleeing into the dense surrounding jungle from which few of them emerged alive. American Special Forces advisors nearly got their asses shot off before being lifted out a few days before the RLA collapse. As there were no Hmong involved Luang Namtha had no effect on what Bill and Pop were doing. Bill's biggest battles continued to be with his fellow Americans who wanted to either horn-in on Momentum or create their own version of it. None of their versions measured up to the original.

Chapter 18: Peace at Last?

By the time the '62 monsoons approached there were rumors of peace in the air. Perhaps even a real peace to replace the 14 months of bogus 'ceasefire' during the Geneva negotiations. On July 23, 1962 Laos was officially at peace, but would it stay at peace? And if so, for how long? Bill Lair was skeptical.

The Geneva Peace Accord of 1962 could have been written by Lewis Carroll. It was as pure a fantasy as *Alice in Wonderland*. The US promised to withdraw all its military and civilian personnel (except diplomats) from Laos, including the CIA. All the people who were not in Laos according to what it had been telling the world for years. Likewise, the Soviet Union, which had also been claiming that it had nobody in Laos and had nothing to do with Kong Le's Neutralist Army, promised to fly its phantom personnel home on the non-existent Ilyushins it had sitting at Neutralist Army HQ on the PDJ. The Peoples Republic of China insisted that its Red Army troops were in Laos on a strictly humanitarian "road building" mission so they didn't have to withdraw. The Democratic Republic of Vietnam, which had staunchly claimed that it had no troops in Laos, declared that it would not withdraw its non-troops until the US removed its advisors from South Vietnam, which had not even been mentioned in the Accord.

These four countries, along with ten others who really didn't have any military or civilian presence in Laos, guaranteed the "Peace and Neutrality of Laos", presumably forever. A Mad Hatter creation christened the Tripartite Government composed of Communists, Neutralists and Right-wing Royalists would rule the new, peaceful, Buddhist, Atheist, Monarchist, Socialist Laos in the name of King Sri Savang Vathana and a rubber-stamp National Assembly to be named later. There was even a berth for the ever-destructive General Phoumi in this Rube Goldberg device of an administration as head of the Rightist faction. He would have to take off his uniform and drop the 'General" bit, not a bad move considering his consistently woeful performance on the battlefield, but he'd still be around to sow his usual mayhem. The cherry on top of this fluffy, wobbly confection would be Prince Souvanna Phouma, the guy the CIA ran out of power to bring in Phoumi. The guy who was now head of the Neutralist faction. The Communists were temporarily pushed into the background but awarded control of key Ministries including Police and Foreign Affairs where they could easily make trouble in the future.

The accord specified that all foreign troops and military advisors must be out of Laos before October 6, 1962. Only foreign diplomats and humanitarian aid workers would be allowed to remain behind. For the US that meant the P.E.O. and Green Berets and Special Forces and White Star Teams...and the CIA, had to go. Bill and Momentum had to pack up and leave. Momentum's future looked doubtful. Bill thought it would be broken up and its staff scattered to the winds. The best that could happen is that it would be tacked onto Bangkok Station as a new, but much diminished, "Laotian Interest Section". Which meant Bill would be back under the thumb of Red Jantzen again. A man he didn't trust and didn't like; and who wanted to get rid of Momentum, and him. Having been given no orders except to get out of Laos he prepared to close his VT operation, cross the Mekong River to Nong Khai, Thailand, and set up there to await further orders. By the October 6 deadline the US had withdrawn all its military personnel totaling the devilish number of 666. The Soviets wouldn't give a number but said all their men were gone. China did nothing while claiming that all the Red Army troops occupying the two Lao provinces on the China border were engaged in humanitarian aid. Hanoi withdrew a token 15 soldiers while leaving 5,000 or so behind in Laos and other thousands waiting in the wings just across the border in North Vietnam. They continued to attack Vang Pao's mountain villages while providing military aid and advisors to the Pathet Lao.

As he was about to make his cross river move, Bill received a cable from CIA HQ giving him permission to leave two agents behind in violation of the peace treaty. They were to be sent to Vang Pao's HQ in Long Cheng to serve in the deepest of deep cover. If their presence was found out it might torpedo the Geneva Accords. Their job would be to send intel provided by VP's spy network, and the Thai PARU Bill had left behind at the various Hmong outposts, to wherever Momentum ended up. Without such info the Agency's Laos screen would go blank as of October 7, 1962. It looked to Bill like his "fairy Godfather" Des Fitzgerald was still watching over him, and Momentum. He had to pick two men to stay behind with Vang Pao and he had to pick 'em quick. He didn't have much to choose from. Jack Shirley would have been his first choice, but after narrowly cheating death at Padong even unflappable Jack wanted out of Laos forever and got himself transferred to Bangkok Station. Bill Young, who had wandered off in search of female company during Padong, had now wandered back. He was a good choice in many ways. He knew the territory and could operate on his own forever if necessary. Nobody knew how long this assignment might last. He was even on friendly terms with VP, or at least he had been until he tried to make a move on VP's youngest, most stunning, and most recent wife. But "The Nature Boy" was way too unpredictable, and too disorganized, for a job like this. An attractive piece of ass might lure him away again, and then where would Bill, and the Agency, be? Tony Poe was a guaranteed disaster on his own...and VP hated him, but if he had a partner who'd keep him under control? Tony Poe and the New Guy? The one who had arrived from CIA Basic just five months ago.

That New Guy was James Vinton Lawrence (1939-2016), who went by 'Vint'. Only barely out of Princeton (Class of '61, BA in Art History, Go Tigers!) and still wet behind the ears, but there was something about him. Something Bill saw in him from the very start. Not the sort of things most people saw in him. The pampered preppy son of a WWII OSS Old Ivy Boy who'd made gazilions in stocks and communed with the high, the mighty, and his fellow members of the social register. The father who counted among his circle of friends both the current DCI and the Secretary of Defense. The golden boy who was clearly on not just the fast, but the meteoric, track in the Agency...if he wanted to be. The very kind of background that should have turned a guy like James William Lair of Bloody Borger, Panhandle High, and Texas A & M, (Go Aggies!) off. But it didn't turn him off.

Bill had been reluctant to take on most of the new help that was continually being thrust upon Momentum, but he had to take some of it. When he did take someone on, they were from one of two extremes; either old guys he knew well, like Pat Landry, or new guys fresh from Agency Basic. He wanted to be their first field assignment so he could put his stamp on them. Imbue them with his personal philosophy of how to operate in Thailand and Laos before they developed any bad habits. He took all his new guys on a strictly 'on trial' basis. 60 days probation, then either in or out. OJT hanging at Momentum's ramshackle HQ plus some free time to roam Vientiane. Informal "instruction" consisting of dinner and drinks at Bill's house in VT. He didn't lecture, merely got conversation started, then sat back twiddling a cigar and waiting for a chance to drive his points home. Words of wisdom combined with a living breathing example of how the end-product of that wisdom worked. Never show anger, never lose control, always polite and deferential, always quiet, always patient, never arguing, never ordering people about, suggesting what might be done, never issuing commands. Learning to speak the language and understand the culture; to understand it and honor it as a legitimate way of life, not an inferior one. Un-American as hell, and Bill knew it, but as far as he was concerned America was in Laos to help the Hmong help us and themselves, not to turn them into proper Americans.

During the long pauses between delivering his pearls of wisdom he watched his new guys through Asiatic-ly averted eyes and listened to their words carefully. He liked everything that he heard and saw of Vint Lawrence. A highly intelligent young man who was eager to learn about his strange new surroundings. A rich kid who showed none of the trappings expected of the privileged classes. No arrogance, no sense of entitlement, no apparent interest in quickly rising to a position of power or fame, no desire except to soak up everything he could learn about the place and time he found himself in and make a good job of whatever tasks came his way. The kid who had grown up poor and humble was meeting the rich humble kid. You don't meet many of those. Bill was impressed. Vint passed his test. He sent young Vint off to fill the most important Agency 'field man' job in Laos, perhaps the most important CIA Case Officer job in Southeast Asia.

Many people questioned Bill's choices. Few of the questioners knew much about new guy, Vint, other than that he was too new, and too green, and didn't meet any of the requirements Bill usually demanded of his field men.

Didn't know Lao or the culture. Was fluent in French and would use it to communicate with VP until he learned enough Lao and Hmong to communicate with him and his men. It didn't take Vint long to learn languages. It didn't take Vint long to learn any of the things he needed to know. Tony Poe drew more criticism than Vint. The only things Bill could say in defense of that decision were that Poe was good at training troops and could get along well in the mountains among the Hmong soldiers even if he rubbed VP the wrong way. A weak argument, especially considering that he'd have few troops to train at Long Cheng. Most of VP's troops had already been trained, and with no "hard rice" airdrops there would be nothing to train them with. If ever Bill could have been accused of making a bad decision this was it.

But that bad decision didn't cost him, or Momentum, because young fair haired Vint Lawrence kept old Tony Poe in line. Kept the obstreperous Tony in line and absorbed Hmong culture like a sponge while becoming VP's best American friend. Learned the languages, both Hmong and Lao. Not only learned all that but still remembered it all in an interview 18 years later that's now on Youtube. He recounts how the two of them flew into Long Cheng via Air America on October 6, 1962 just ahead of the Geneva Accords deadline. Once their lift departed, they were the only two CIA agents left in Laos. Everyone else was gone. They were in Laos illegally though with the secret permission of the Director of Central Intelligence, who would surely deny ever giving that permission if they were discovered.

Vint and Tony were told to keep their heads down. The ICC's (International Control Commission) white helicopters flew over Long Cheng almost every day. They could have landed if they had wanted to, but they never did. Air America flights were cut back and were only allowed to deliver rice and medicine. V and T had to get by on their own. No idea how long they were going to be there. Could be years. Like being stranded on a desert island. Vint had his own house but took all his meals with Vang Pao at his place. Always at least 15 or 20 people squatting round the low table. Different mixture of characters every meal. Always some new faces, people wandering in from remote villages. VP knew them all. Lots of eating and drinking. Seemingly endless conversation. The Hmong were nothing like the lowland Lao. Lots of joking around. Raucous laughter. Disputes and arguments. No polite smiles and deference and feigned agreement that signified nothing. The Hmong always said what they meant. They would have been right at home with the Mountain Men of the American Wild West. VP was both the political and military leader of the Hmong. Vint was in awe of his political skills. Said no one else could lead such a fiercely independent and fractious people. 18 clans each one of which behaved like they were law unto themselves. Clans, and hierarchies within clans. VP had five wives, each one carefully selected from important families, but that was only the beginning of his byzantine political apparatus. The Hmong had been driven out of China into northern Vietnam in the early 1800's, then driven out of Vietnam in the late 1800's. They had developed a loose organization to resist the Vietnamese before Ho Chi Minh was born. An organization that VP had to keep alive. That organization had been centered on the Plain of Jars which was now in NVA hands. And if that wasn't bad enough already there were many thousands of Hmong who lived in villages so isolated that they had never been part of the PDJ organization. And all the Hmong were being chased around by the Vietnamese...and Bill Lair's Momentum support was now cut off indefinitely, or perhaps forever. No help from the outside, including the Royal Lao Government (RLG). The King of Laos had pledged an eternal alliance with the Hmong in the early 1900's giving Hmong Country a sort of autonomy, but no assistance beyond that.

Vint called his job at Long Cheng "hand-holding". Being a fly on the wall at every meal. A fly on the wall at every meeting VP had with his spies, or anyone who had information to bring him. A quiet observer at the occasional large semi-formal meetings of his commanders and clan leaders. Vint went along with him on his trips to surrounding villages. Trips that had to be made on foot as there were no aircraft to take them. VP called Vint his son and treated him like one. He described VP as "a charismatic leader, dynamic and brilliant, a true man of the common people who understood those people from the ground up, who knew their psychology". Eventually he would see VP in military as well as political action and called him "a great and inspiring guerilla battlefield commander who did not understand grand strategy because it was outside the realm of his experience." Vint would stay on with VP at Long Cheng for five years. He would come to know more about the Hmong than any American, more even than Bill Lair, who he admired every bit as much as Vang Pao. In 1980 he would call those five years the most exciting years of his life. The years that taught him more about life, and human nature, than all the rest of his life put together.

With its two deep cover positions filled, it didn't take long for Bill's outfit to quit VT. There were only a handful of Americans and some HQ PARU to pull out. Nong Khai was a pleasant place. A small sleepy provincial capital straggling along the steep banks of the mighty Mekong with a well-kept Buddhist Temple every few blocks. Government buildings Siamese Victorian instead of French Colonial. Restaurants hanging precariously out over the crumbling riverbank where you could take in a sweeping view of the mile-wide Mekong and watch the ferry boats arc back and forth across it breasting its powerful current. Plain comfortable surroundings with cold beer and top-notch food. Bill's kind of town. What's not to like? One big thing, so it proved. Nong Khai was not the place for a clandestine operation like Momentum. The only other white faces in town were a couple of missionaries. Talk about sticking out like a sore thumb! They had an audience for everything they did that followed them everywhere they went. Vientiane was positively teeming with big white farangs compared to Nong Khai. Too bad but it wasn't gonna' work out. Next stop Udorn.

Chapter 19: Ugly Udorn

Momentum's new HQ lacked the somewhat seedy charm of Vientiane. In truth it lacked all charm either seedy or otherwise. Only a decade or so before Momentum's arrival in late '62 it had been little more than a village called Ban Makkhang (mock keng) named after a tree that bares a small bitter fruit much prized by Isan Thais (and by the Hmong who have smuggled some of the seeds into my home state of Minnesota where the trees they planted are doing quite well). A tree that grows wild flourishing in the boggy soil of what is now downtown Udorn. It must have been those trees that attracted Udorn's first settlers. There was no other reason to establish a village that grew into a gritty little city at the bottom of a natural bowl which collects rainfall from miles around. There were only two seasons in Udorn in 1962. Flood season and recovering from flood season. The town was perpetually grimy, shabby, and pungent. Its water was unsafe to drink or bathe in. Cholera was a seasonal threat, malaria a permanent threat. The only thing good about Udorn was its people. The tough hardworking determined-to-survive people of Isan. Many of those who had fled the 4-year drought that chased General Phibun and brought in Marshall Sarit in 1957 were still around scratching for a living in "the Big Makkhang" in 1962. There was some money to made, not much, but more than was to be made in their home villages where the only cash to be seen was the one-baht (5 cents) banknotes with the image of the King tacked in a position of honor on the wall of every house.

But things were looking up. The rains had returned. Crops were good. The US-financed Friendship Highway (Thanon Mitraphab) had reached town. With the highway and the Royal Thai Railway also recently completed Udorn was connected to the outside world for the first time in its history. The US Strategic Air Command had built an air strip in 1952 that became a Royal Thai Air Force Base. Civil Air Transport, Air America's predecessor, showed up in 1955 with three C-46's to run cargo airdrops around Southeast Asia, but it wasn't until Kong Le's 1960 coup in Laos than any substantial American presence was felt. Aerial recon flights were being run out of Udorn by early

'61. A 300-man Marine chopper outfit called Airbase Squadron 16 soon followed. By May of '62, with the defeat of Phoumi's RLA at Luang Namtha, the US ante was upped to include 20 Marine A-4 Skyhawks from the Philippines and more choppers, plus Marine ground troops. Deployment of a whole Marine Brigade was being booted about as WWIII loomed across the Mekong 35 miles away. Then in July the Geneva Peace Accords were signed and the panic subsided. Within a month the hastily assembled US forces departed even faster than they had arrived. Not long after they left, Bill and his Momentum crew popped in.

The crew found Udorn RTAFB a near ghost town when they showed up. A single squadron of Thai T-28's (the venerable WWII pilot trainer that became a jury-rigged bomber in SE Asia) with a commander who flew his plane open cockpit wearing a long scarf that trailed behind him in the wind like a WWI ace (or the cartoon character Snoopy), and CAT/Air America's by now somewhat larger fleet of equally antique transports. That was about it. The Agency owned a drab featureless wooden building near the runway which was rendered effectively windowless by air-conditioners mounted in each of its few windows. It had aerials sprouting from its roof as any good CIA facility should have, and a radio room inside. It had been lightly used by visiting spooks from several countries, most notably Taiwan, as a temporary intercept base. A perfect fit, ready for occupancy, partially furnished, no assembly required, no nosy neighbors, plenty of security provided with the package. Plus, a bonus Bill Lair had been pining for for ages, a promotion, his first in the 12-plus years since he joined the Agency. His first in the 11-plus years since he set foot in Thailand. He was now Chief of the 4802nd Joint Liaison Detachment, Udorn, with a civilian GS rank equivalent to Lieutenant Colonel. Finally, a bit of well-deserved recognition. And what was even better, he reported to Vientiane Station, not to his old nemesis BKK Station "Red". A bare bones VT Station now that had remained in Laos disguised as Embassy staff.

A happy Bill Lair reported to work at 7 each morning, 7 days a week. On his desk he found the latest radio messages from CIA HQ-now in its grand new Langley digs, Vientiane Station, his "Man in Long Cheng" Vint Lawrence, and his scattered PARU teams in the misty mountains of Laos. He and Pat Landry had their desks pushed together so they faced each other as they read cables and discussed them back and forth trying to understand the ever-shifting military and political winds of Laos. There was always a stream of questions that needed to be answered. Always thorny problems that had to be pondered over. With the day's most pressing problems disposed of Bill occasionally went off to visit his friend, PARU co-commander, fellow Thai Police Lieutenant Colonel, and now also Chief of Thai Headquarters 333 which would come to control all Thai forces in Laos, Pranet Ritruechai, at his office. Once a month he made a trip to PARU HQ in Hua Hin, though the multi-talented Pranet now also ran PARU's day-to-day operations. Bill was too busy with Laos to pay much attention to what PARU continued to do in Thailand. Most days Bill stuck around until dinnertime, then he and Pat and any other spooks who wanted to join them left base for a meal at a Thai restaurant, after which Bill and the workaholic Pat returned to labor for a few more hours. The two of them did some of their best thinking in the evenings when there were few people around, no one except them and the guys in the "radio shack". It was then that they put aside the day's details and looked at the Big Picture.

****

Author's note: I can't say for a fact that Bill and his fellow spooks frequented a Thai restaurant in Udorn called "The Three Sisters" during 1962-68, but I like to think they did. It was a favorite hangout of Ramasun Station spooks when I was there 1968-71. Looked like it had been around for quite a while then. It is still around now (as of 2019, I just checked with my Thai stepson Sunthorn to make sure). The only classy eatery in Udorn. Always crowded. You could wind your way up to a second-floor mezzanine to look down on the noisy animated crowds or dine intimately in one of the small private dining rooms in the rear of the establishment. I didn't know anything about Bill Lair the last time I ate there in 2017. Now that I do, I'm going to pay special attention when my Thai relatives and I convene in one of those dining rooms next time I'm in Udorn. Maybe I'll spot the ghost of Bill Lair quietly smiling in one of the corners. Be sure to order the hot and spicy pork with cashews, the nuts are fresh from trees not more than 20 miles away. Bon appetite!

Bill, who had originally thought the "fairy tale" peace of Geneva would be a bummer, now liked what he saw happening in Laos. VP's guerilla operations were suspended due to lack of "hard rice", but so were the operations of the PL and NVA, at least for the moment. Putting VP on a diet of limited supplies might keep him from becoming too dependent on US largesse. Bill's combined PARU teams and the two secret CIA guys at Long Cheng were roughly the size of outfit he'd wanted in the first place. It's intel gathering capabilities were better than they'd ever been. He didn't have to slug it out with all the military types who wanted to horn in on his action, or take it over, as they'd all gotten the boot. No more White Star Teams or Special Forces or Green Berets...good riddance to the lot of 'em. And, much to his surprise, Udorn proved to be a better home for his clandestine operation than Vientiane or Nongkhai. No need to play spy in UDN. You could use your own name and move freely about without fear that someone might try to take a shot you. No panicky VT Station Chiefs or bossy American Ambassadors to spoil your day. Bill knew the Thai Police so well that he couldn't have gotten arrested if he'd tried. He was even closer to his family than he had been. His highborn Thai wife wouldn't have been caught dead in a dump like Udorn, but it was much easier for him to visit her and his two children in Bangkok than it had been in VT. Bill never said much about his wife and family. It appears that they led largely separate lives during Bill's years in Southeast Asia. He seemed to prefer a bachelor's life, and even if he hadn't, the kind of work he did would have kept him separated from his family most of the time. Bill visited them in Bangkok regularly once a month. They never visited him in Udorn.

Chapter 20: War Returns to Laos on not-so-little Cat's Feet

Anyone who was paying attention knew that the flimsy structure called the Geneva Peace Accord of 1962 would be swept away by the first strong breeze, but many, including Bill Lair, hoped it would survive a gentle breeze for at least a while. He ushered in the New Year of 1963 by sneakily dispatching a gift of a half-ton each of spam, beans and rice to his men Vint and Tony in Long Cheng. Vittles that came courtesy of the Bay of Pigs debacle whose troops weren't in the field long enough to eat them. The PL and NVA, who had paid no attention to the 14-month cease-fire during which the Accords were negotiated, promptly blew them off. They started slowly nibbling here and there at widely scattered Hmong village outposts. VP fumed that he couldn't resist the enemy without "hard rice". Even threatened to quit Momentum. Bill realized that was an idle threat. If he didn't stay with Momentum where would he go? Still he was worried too. If the Communists pushed hard enough and long enough the Hmong would eventually need "hard rice". For the present all he could do was forward the increasing number of treaty violation messages he received from the hand-cranked radio sets of his PARU teams via Vint's daily SITREP (Situation Report) to Langley and hope they could do something about them. He knew Des Fitzgerald would be doing his damnedest to get them noticed, and acted on, but he didn't know what Des was up against; or rather who he was up against.

Des was locked in mortal combat with "The Crocodile", Ambassador-without-portfolio Averill Harriman, the George Washington of the 1962 Geneva Accords. With his deliberately heavy-lidded supercilious glare he was as dangerous as the mightiest, and oldest, of crocs. And he was not about to let anybody mess with his diplomatic masterpiece. He considered "The Laos Problem" solved and had already moved on to more important things, like what would soon become the Vietnam War. He knew about Vang Pao and his Hmong. He knew about Bill Lair and his Operation Momentum. He knew what a pain in the ass the boys from Hanoi were. He knew about everything. He was a master of detail. To "The Crocodile" Vang Pao and his Hmong people were expendable. So were Bill Lair and his Momentum people. All of them pawns on his Southeast Asia chessboard, but now there more important pieces, and moves, to be considered.

By February of 1963 the PL and NVA began to move beyond 'nibbling' to more serious treaty violations. Kong Le's Neutralist Army had been the Joker in the Laos deck ever since it toppled Phoumi in 1960. No one was ever sure whose side it was on. Often the diminutive paratrooper didn't seem to be sure himself. Shunned by the Americans and courted by the Communists at first, then courted by both sides later, he didn't know what to do. Diplomatic maneuvering was beyond his grasp. Accused of being a Communist, though he wasn't one, he had to side with somebody to keep his army from falling apart. At first, he signed on with both the Soviets and North Vietnamese. He would have preferred to take only the Russians because they had the supplies he desperately needed and could deliver them, but apparently it was a package deal. The Viets didn't have much of anything to offer him beyond the threat that if he didn't sign with them, they'd attack him. The Soviets made good on their part of the bargain. Airlifted his troops up to Xiengkhouangville on the PDJ and delivered all the WWII surplus guns ammo and supplies he required. The Viets didn't make good on much beyond their threats. On February 12, 1963 things began to turn nasty. Somebody, most likely the PL, assassinated Colonel Ketsana Vongsavong at his home not far from Neutralist HQ. Ketsana was a good friend and staunch supporter of Kong Le who then possibly avenged himself by having Laos' left-leaning Foreign Minister Quinim Pholsena assassinated at his home in Vientiane on April 1. If he didn't do it, many people at least thought he did it. Rumor was spreading that KL was about to switch sides and go American. The Soviets seemed to be even more confused and unpredictable than KL. They were now in a mood to quit Laos altogether; which threated to cut off KL's supplies. The PL had lured some of the Neutralists into their camp and these "new" Neutralists began clashing with KL's "old" Neutralists. By the end of March KL had had enough. He broke with both the PL and NVA; and moved his HQ 50 miles northeast along Highway 7 to Muong Soui to get clear of them.

By mid-April Hmong irregulars and villagers were bringing word to PARU radio men that the Communists were on the move. Behind their usual screen of PL advance-men they were bound east across the PDJ headed for Muong Soui. Their intent was obvious. They already had KL's righthand man in their pocket and anointed him commander of the "new" Neutralist Army. A coup against coup-sters was underway. Vang Pao decided that he had to act. If the Communists took Moung Soui they'd be right square in his front yard; poised to menace tens of thousands of Hmong villagers; a clear and present danger to his Long Cheng HQ itself. Bill Lair, Vint and Tony decided to act regardless of what The Crocodile had decreed. Even "Whitey" Whitehurst the VT Station Chief was covertly on board. The Croc's Geneva Accords were nothing but a crock, a complicated charade from their very beginning. Even the International Control Commission (ICC) that was supposed to be enforcing the rules was part of that charade. The Agency might as well get into the act too. But time was of the essence. The PL and NVA were coming on fast and they didn't have that far to go. Bill and VP sketched out a rough battle plan. VP's men would place the 75-mm pack howitzers they already had, and some new rockets the CIA would send them, on a mountaintop that commanded the approach the NVA would have to take to reach Moung Soui. Hmong troops would be brought in by Air America H-34 choppers. Tony instructed the Hmong on how to operate the rockets, which were fired from steel racks. The hastily staged performance was not ready for prime time. VP insisted on trying to steal the show. His supposed skills as an artillerist proved to be non-existent. His troops skills weren't much better. Luckily all the bing-bam-boom, especially from the rockets that the enemy had never been under before, scared them away. For once the friendlies could have used Tony Poe on the scene, but Bill barred Tony and Vint from leaving Long Cheng.

The reason the Hmong were such poor artillerists was they didn't believe in gravity. They couldn't understand that a projectile arced when fired long distances. All their hunting and ambushing had been done at close quarters as there wasn't enough open ground in the dense jungles of Hmong Country

to see, or shoot, farther. They were great shots at short range with direct-fire weapons but hopeless with howitzers and rockets at long range. Eventually some of them learned about gravity and the curvature of the earth, which they thought was flat, but it took a while. Centuries of firmly fixed beliefs don't disappear overnight, not in Hmong Country or anywhere else.
****

Author's note: VP's bombardment, despite its muddled execution, saved the Laotian Neutralist Army, or at least most of it. I became the Laotian Translation Section's Neutralist specialist by default in 1969. None of my fellow Lao "lingies" (interpreters) wanted the job. By then they were on our side. After VP's artillerists who couldn't shoot straight spooked them in '63 the PL and NVA set up their own version of the Neutralist Army under the command of their man Colonel Deuan Sipaseuth. They were still around in 1969 as the Deuanist Neutralists. In addition, the Chinese got their oar in and conjured up their own captive Neutralists under an elderly political Colonel (who they promoted to General, of course) named Khammouane Boupha. He was reportedly still around in 1969 as well as the head of the Khammouanist Neutralists. We never intercepted evidence of either of these forces being present on a battlefield, but both were frequently mentioned on the propaganda broadcasts of The Voice of the Freedom Loving Peoples of Laos which were beamed in from Kunming, China. The "old" Kong Le Neutralists, however, did survive, and fight. And, in addition to fighting, they protected the Neutralist Faction's Prime Minister Souvanna Phouma from many a right-wing coup. They claimed to have 10,000 troops in 1970. Probably had 6-7,000.

Hardly anyone in VT knew what had happened on the road to Moung Soui. It was part of the secret war within The Secret War. The striped pants boys at the US Embassy didn't know about it. They didn't know about much of anything that happened in the mountainous 85% of Laos. One of them, Charles Stevenson, wrote a book called *American Policy Toward Laos Since 1954* which provides an exhaustive, and exhausting, history of all the diplomatic comings and goings in the little Kingdom but doesn't mention Operation Momentum and contains only one brief reference to Bill Lair. It provides only enough info about the "Meo" to verify their existence, but little beyond that. In Stevenson's diplomatic world of Laos things were still chugging right along. The Tripartite Government of Laos, which was feebly operational as of August 27, 1962 was doing fine. The country was at peace because his big boss Averill Harriman insisted it was at peace. CIA's Des Fitzgerald continued to send his luckless Deputy Bill Colby (who would later rise to DCI) off with fresh reports of Communist ceasefire violations regularly. No doubt Colby dragged himself to Harriman's office with news of the Neutralist coup-within-a-coup and the subsequent PL/NVA move on Muong Soui only to receive the standard greeting which was one of the Crocs' lordly patented insults. Harriman was justly famous for his icy insults throughout Washington.

By late April '63, however, cracks in the peaceful façade of Laos were becoming visible even to the VT crowd. The "Red Prince" Souphanouvong, leader of the Communist faction of the Tri-P government, had stormed out of VT following the assassination of Foreign Minister Quinim contending that he was no longer safe in the city. His half-brother Neutralist Prime Minister Souvanna Phouma tried to coax him back but to no avail. It would be many years before the Red Prince returned to VT. The Tripartite Government of Laos-fourteen months in negotiation and one month in formation, was effectively dead after eight months of operation. Averill Harriman would never admit that his Geneva Accords had turned to mush but now it didn't matter. The CIA was already secretly making an end run around him with a guy who he would have regarded as pond scum, Bill Lair, as their point man. The Croc was elevated to Deputy Secretary of State in early May and replaced by Roger Hilsman. Rog didn't stick around for long, but the WWII OSS Old Burma Boy was behind the desk long enough to give the Agency the green light for what he already knew they were doing in Laos. By June the National Security Council (NSC) made it (secretly) official. It continued to bar the US military from Laos while ignoring the Geneva restrictions on "hard rice". In somewhat related news during that same month the Russians packed up and left Laos. Nobody could figure out just why they left, including, apparently, themselves.

Bill and Momentum were back in the paramilitary business as the sole American outlet in Laos. It wouldn't be long before they got their first big order. In early August of 1963 the NSC 'required' them to disrupt NVA truck traffic on a section of Highway 7 that wound from the border of North Vietnam along the west edge of the PDJ and eventually reached the Republic of South Vietnam. The NVA had been using what would come to be called the Ho Chi Minh Trail to send troops and supplies to South Vietnam ever since 1959 when they began to improve old footpaths into motorable roads. By '63 those roads were the best in Laos and the Hanoi Trucking Company was a well-run, well-organized operation. Shutting down that operation would be a big job and Bill Lair would be the first American to get a crack at it. It may not have fit his hit-and-run guerilla model all that well, but he thought he could find a way to do it without interfering with his "regular" Hmong business.

The most vulnerable chunk of Highway 7 was a 25-mile stretch between the villages of Nakhang and Ban Ban. The road there skirted the northwest edge of the PDJ clinging to the side of its steep slopes. Most of it could be viewed from the flat top of Bouam Long Mountain which was one of the original "Seven Fortress" mountains that Vang Pao revealed to Pop Buell in their meeting of December 12, 1960. Bill consulted with demolition experts at the Udorn Airbase to formulate a plan built around the use of cratering charges to blast the road clean off the mountainside. This was to be by far the most complicated mission ever undertaken by VP's Hmong army. The charges would have to be airdropped in heavily padded boxes via the same kind of parabolic winged 24-foot cargo parachutes Bill and PARU had tested at Hua Hin years before. Six-foot deep holes would have to be dug into the hard gravel roadbed at fifteen-foot intervals following a zig-zag pattern. A glob of C-4 plastique had to be fixed onto each charge as a booster along with a detonator. Then the whole thing had to be carefully covered with dirt. It was an operation that required a lot of preparation, a lot of training, and a lot of men. Men and aircraft to 'chute in the charges, men to dig the holes and plant the charges, men to keep the enemy at bay while the charges were being planted and readied. This wasn't going to be a quick hit-and-run in-and-out operation. It would take a long time to get things ready for the big boom. A PARU team ran a demonstration for the Hmong at Long Cheng, then worked with Vang Pao's officers to get things perfectly straight. Tony Poe knew plenty about cratering charges and C-4 but was reduced to spectator as the PARU guys did their thing. PARU teams would lead the operation backed by 12 platoon-sized units of carefully selected elite Hmong troops. There would be no Americans on the ground. Not even Tony, though he would be overhead circling around in an Air America plane dropping radio-guided chute-loads of destruction to those on the ground. When all was ready one dark night the whole thing went off in an enormous bang that echoed round the mountainsides above and the flatlands below. Two lengthy sections of Highway 7 vanished. Bright and early the next morning a surveillance plane flew over the road to take some pictures. One of those pictures caught a knot of PL soldiers staring down from a dead-ended Highway 7 wondering where it had gone. In the span of just a couple of weeks Bill, and the PARU, and the Hmong, and Air America, had mounted a complex operation with many moving parts...and none of those parts went wrong! Since the attack was pulled off in the middle of the monsoon season it took the Viets many months to get their Trail repaired. It would be not only the longest, but the only, time the Trail was completely shut down.

The remainder of 1963 was pretty much more of the same. The political situation continued to deteriorate. Bill Lair, now armed with the NSC's favorable ruling, continued to expand Momentum taking it in some new directions. Soon there were so many varieties of "paramilitaries" in Laos that you couldn't tell the players without a program. There were the "plain vanilla" Hmong village militia, sometimes also called the ADC after their old French predecessor the Auto Defense de Choc. The new Special Guerilla Units (SGU's) that came in varying sizes and configurations. Everything from Battalion Size (300 men or so) units of mixed Hmong and Lao troops, to company-size, to platoon-size. The village militias were the home guard, defending their turf and ambushing any enemy who wandered into their area. The SGU's were the mobile "shock troops" sent where needed, usually by chopper, better trained and armed...and much better paid. And in South Laos something completely new. Sometimes called SGUs, sometimes called Trail-watchers. Not Hmong at all but a tribal group politely called the Lao Theung (hill country Lao) or more usually the Kha (slaves). Living at 1500 to

2500-foot elevations of the southern half of Laos they are the only truly "native" Lao. Everybody else is from somewhere else, mostly from China. It's just a question of how long ago they got to Laos, which is anywhere from 2,000 years ago to yesterday. The Lao Theung are not known to be fighters like the Hmong, but they are known for their hunting and tracking skills. Lowland Lao say that you will never see a Kha unless he wants you to see him. Which is the same thing the Thais said about the Karen in the jungles behind Hua Hin. Bill didn't try to turn them into fighters. He used them to their, and his, best advantage as spies. His headquarters for them in Savannakhet and Pakse were more like drop-in centers where they could come to town, spill their information, draw some necessaries, and bed down for a while before returning to the jungle. He modelled Momentum's South Laos operation on the Young family's informal spy net home base in Chieng Mai that yielded so much info about the goings-on in the Kunming Military Region (KMR), that large area of Southwest China bordering on Burma, Thailand and Laos. The KMR was so top secret that even Chinese citizens needed a special security clearance to set foot in it. Bill Lair's Lao Theung "watchers" were equally useful in South Laos.

****

Author's note: I've never heard the Lao Theung called anything but the Kha in Laos or Northeast Thailand. They are said to be related to the Aborigines of Australia. People who display physical features like frizzy or even wavy hair, thick lips, flattened noses, "red" hair (meaning a rusty red-brown color), or a particular curl at the corners of their eyes, are said to have "Kha blood". My wife says her father was part Kha. He came from the hill country of Laos. He was dead before I met her, so I never saw him, but he was a locally renowned hunter and woodsman. My Thai stepson Sunthorn has slightly 'red' naturally wavy hair, something no "real" Thai or Lao ever has according to "the experts"; so maybe she's right.

Chapter 21: New Year, New Problems

1964 began well for Bill Lair and his highly irregular outfit. They were still the only American military game in town. The usual "regulars" were chomping at the bit to get back in the door but the NSC's edict of the previous June applied only to the CIA and it still stood. In early January Bill went back to the States for the first time in five years to meet with that august Council. He was perhaps the lowest ranking CIA officer ever to appear before it. Still they wanted to hear from him. Wanted to know more about Momentum and its successes. Wanted to know more about the Hmong. Especially their leader Vang Pao. Wanted to know if there were any others like him to fill his shoes if he was killed, or overthrown. Bill assured them that there were, and that VP was unlikely to be ousted. That he had several capable junior officers who could take his place. That he had no significant political opposition. They were glad to hear it. They had been hearing quite a lot of bad news about the war in Southeast Asia. Some of that news even came from Washington.

A grand Southeast Asia wargame devised by the prestigious Rand Corporation that simulated a 10-year conflict between the Blues (USA) and Reds (North Vietnam, USSR, PRC) had been fought out in the nation's Capital. The game ended in a Red victory that left 500,000 defeated US troops on the ground. The Red triumph hinged on their ability and willingness to take heavy casualties and extend the conflict until the Blue Team tired of it. Tired of it and concluded that while they were busy fighting it the Reds were eating their lunch elsewhere. The cost of those simulated ten years was enormous. Better to stay small and cheap and "deniable, reversible, easy-in easy-out" like Laos' Momentum in Bill Lair's very own words. Those were the kind of words the National Security Council wanted to hear in January of 1964. Unfortunately, later National Security Councils proved deaf to those same words. Another, later, study, estimated that the cost of running the Vietnam War was 700 times the cost of the Secret War in Laos. A rather high price to pay for "American boots on the ground" openness. The guy who played the role of General Giap for the Reds was William H. Sullivan. The same Bill Sullivan who would become Ambassador to Laos before the year was out.

But, by that time he seems to have forgotten the lessons of his starring role in Omega. When Bill Lair returned to Ugly Udorn in February he found bad news of his own waiting for him. The PL and NVA having rebuilt the vaporized sections of Highway 7 had resupplied and were on the offensive. In a dry season push that lasted until April they overran several of VP's ADC village outposts. The 'see' part of the see-saw war over the PDJ was already underway. Momentum would have to gear up to launch the 'saw' part later in the year. Bill might be in line for some help by then. The more conventional military types had decided that if he could run Momentum from Udorn they could run some of their own Laos operations from the same place.

First to get off the ground (pardon the pun) was a program to train Lao pilots to fly the sturdy WWII T-28 and AT-6 Texan trainers turned bombers. The Royal Laotian Air Force (RLAF) was about to be born. To hasten its delivery some already trained and experienced RTAF Thai pilots were added to the mix. The sort of trick they might well have learned from Bill's PARU. While the RLAF was preparing to take wings politics as usual continued in VT, or rather military coups as usual. This time it wasn't Phoumi but his sometime sidekick MR5 Commander Kouprasith Abhay who staged the coup. At 6-4 and 300+ pounds "Fat K" was the RLA's biggest General, and his daughter Viendara was certainly the tallest woman in Laos. She stood an even six feet, was gorgeous, and didn't weigh anywhere near 300 pounds. I went out with her once when I was studying Lao in DC. She was a family friend of my Lao teacher. Had come to the States looking for a tall husband. At 6-5 I qualified. Unfortunately, I was also a PFC frozen in grade for the duration of my 47-week Lao course before I would be eligible for elevation to Specialist 4th Class so it didn't work out. She found herself a Lt. Colonel. He was a couple of inches shorter than me, but his higher rank more than made up the difference. Oh, and her father's coup failed. (And I married a woman who is 4-11 on tip-toe).

By May '64 the USAF was flying recon flights from Thailand over the Ho Chi Minh Trail. They weren't bombing it yet, but they were getting ready to. By June Thai pilots flying on behalf of the RLAF were dropping some bombs in support of VP's troops on the PDJ. Bill had never been keen on bombing. He certainly remembered all the American troops he'd see killed by errant American bombs during his WWII days. He'd almost been one of them. When the zoomies (USAF guys) started talking 'surgical airstrikes' he was decidedly skeptical. But bombs delivered by old slow-moving piston-pounders in close contact with spotters on the ground were near enough to 'surgical' to suit him, and a new wrinkle to Momentum strategy was added.

The RLA even won one of its rare battles in July of '64. With the NVA pulling its troops back for the monsoons it defeated the left-behind PL at the Sala Phou Khoun junction of Highways 7 and 13 50-odd very winding miles south of Luang Prabang and reopened the road from VT to that fair (it really is fair) city for the first time in two years for those equipped with barf-buckets to make the sickening and dangerous journey.

By October the US was helping the Thai-and-Lao piloted RLAF bomb the Ho Chi Minh Trail. It was the beginning of the American bombing. By December '64 the American bombing of the Trail ramped up with President Lyndon B. Johnson's approval. On December 14 that bombing was expanded to northern Laos, Hmong Country. A new and very destructive phase of the Secret War in Laos was beginning. It would become much harder to keep that war secret from now on.

Chapter 22: The Field Marshall and the Kennedy Letter

Bill Sullivan, who had acquitted himself so well in the role of General Ngo Dinh Giap in the widely discussed production called Omega arrived in VT during the tag end of 1964 as the new US Ambassador to Laos replacing Leonard Unger. At about the same time the CIA replaced "Whitey" Whitehurst with a new Vientiane Station Chief, Douglas Blaufarb. Change was in the air in Laos. No one yet knew if it would be change for the better, or for the worse.

Back in May of 1961 the newly elected President John F. Kennedy wrote a letter to all US Ambassadors telling them how he wanted them to handle Communist insurgencies. His recommendations were heavily influenced by the theories of Brigadier General Edward G. Lansdale (1908-87) which had been widely discussed and very popular since the late-1950s. The core of Lansdale's theory was the "Country Team" concept. That all US agencies in a threatened country should co-ordinate their efforts and work together under the direction of the US Ambassador who would be Team Leader. In more specific language the President ordered that all Ambassadors "be assigned clear primacy to direct all counter-insurgency efforts in their countries" and should "have the power to direct and coordinate all operations." That they could do everything short of commanding US troops in the field.

How they accomplished that "direction and coordination" was up to them. JFK gave them no instruction in that regard. All the members of the 'Team' had their own headquarters to direct them. Did the President's letter eliminate that direction? Was each US Ambassador now effectively running the CIA, and USAID, and all the Military Services, and all the other assorted US agencies in his country? In practice that came to depend on the nature of the man who filled the job of Ambassador. Many continued in the traditional way. Keeping in touch with the heads of the various agencies. Giving them direction from time to time, even negotiating with them, but basically letting them do what their HQ's wanted them to do so long as they kept him informed of what they were up to. Others formed Country Teams composed of the heads of the various agencies which met regularly to discuss and coordinate their activities.

In Laos Bill Sullivan's predecessors had followed the traditional approach of "keep me informed" supplemented by occasional all-agencies get togethers. Sullivan came in with what might be called the Genghis Khan approach to "direction and coordination." Daily meetings at the Embassy of all agency heads which he presided over with an iron hand. Quick removal of anyone who didn't toe his line. "Discussions" in which he dictated while the rest of the Team took notes and kept their mouths shut. He was quickly tagged "The Field Marshall" and gloried in that nickname. Sullivan, whose early State Department career had been hampered by his pushy, outspoken, aggressive, abrasive nature was now in what he considered his proper element...and a lot of other people were in a world of hurt. He would push the old Kennedy Letter to its limits and beyond. The man who served in WWII as a gunnery officer on a destroyer would eventually muscle his way into command of something infinitely more destructive than a 5-inch gun. But mountainous Laos was not the Pacific Ocean and his service as an armchair military strategist would prove to be far less than successful.

Sullivan knew just enough about Laos to make himself dangerous. He had been plucked out of obscurity by none other than the old "Crocodile" Averill Harriman who put him on the negotiating team he headed to whip up the frothy Geneva Accords of 1962. The Croc must have seen the rude supercilious insanely ambitious Sullivan as himself thirty years younger. A man who made few friends and many enemies but ramrodded things through. He would prove to be as calculating and cold-blooded and unforgiving to his enemies, both real and imagined, as the Croc himself. He would preserve the façade of Harriman's masterful Accords for the next five years even though those Accords had effectively become fiction long before he arrived in Vientiane knowing more about the land of peoples of Switzerland than he did about Laos.

The arrival of the "Field Marshall" had no immediate effect on Bill Lair and Operation Momentum. Bill wasn't counted as an Agency Chief, so he didn't have to attend Sullivan's mandatory daily meetings. Being considered a mere "field hand" by someone like the Field Marshall was not that bad of a thing. There were also advantages to being headquartered in a place that nobody of authority, including his own wife, wanted to visit. Besides that, Bill Sullivan had his hands full during his first months "in command". In February 1965 there was yet another military coup. Coups were an annual event in Laos. A monsoon season and a coup season. This one boasted a particularly impressive cast of co-conspirators. "Fat K", General Kouprasith, once again took the leading role with the ever-conspiratorial Phoumi not far behind and a star-studded cast of a half-dozen bemedaled notables including the commanders of several elite RLA units. The US Embassy usually worked from the sidelines in such cases, but Sullivan plunged into the thick of the action with heartening success. The coup was put down without bloodshed and there was even a big bonus. Phoumi was exiled to Thailand never to return.

Meanwhile Bill Lair and his PARU teams were quietly helping Vang Pao's men chase the PL and NVA from the outposts they'd overrun in early 1964. Having accomplished that task, they turned to a hit-and-run campaign to harass the PL and NVA on their home turf of Sam Neua Province. They found such enthusiastic support among the Sam Neua Hmong that they turned their harassment into an offensive which penetrated all the way to the edge of Sam Neua Town. There they uncovered a huge NVA Headquarters Complex. Buried deep in a labyrinth of limestone karst caves impervious to US bombing it contained vast stores of food and munitions as well as voluminous files. Even caverns stacked with the diaries of dead NVA soldiers that had not been sent to their next of kin. Bill flew up to inspect the massive haul. Ever the anti-bureaucrat he was amused by the underground ocean of paperwork kept by the meticulous Vietnamese. It must have taken my Vietnamese lingy comrades ages to dig through it all. The guns and ammo found in the caves were destroyed. The Hmong residents of Sam Neua Province lived high off the hog on NVA provisions for a long time. It was the ultimate insult to North Vietnamese power and organization. The Hmong, and by extension via Momentum, the USA, were hardly more than a hundred miles from Hanoi reading their records; and their PL comrades were exposed as the punch-less puppets that they and their window-dressing government had always been.

On a high after his Sam Neua triumph Bill was brought down to earth by his first encounter with The Field Marshall. Having escaped the FM's bloody claws for six months he considered himself lucky based on what he'd heard from some of those who had suffered through his meetings. The previous Ambassador Leonard Unger had given Bill permission to call up planes and direct airstrikes in case of emergencies. For six months he'd had nothing he considered an emergency. On May 20, 1965 he finally had one. A pilot for Bird & Sons, an Air America contractor, made a delivery to a Lima site in Hmong Country that had just been overrun by the enemy. A little later another pilot spotted the abandoned aircraft on the ground and radioed Momentum HQ at Udorn. The control freak Field Marshall now had his Embassy radio operators monitoring the transmissions of other US Agencies and called the CIA to see if the pilot was dead. Meanwhile Bill had jumped into the fastest plane available and headed for the Lima site calling in American piloted T-28s, a Caribou to circle the site to provide radio relays, and an Air America chopper to land and see what was happening. The chopper pilot feared landing, but the toughest of Bill's tough Thai PARU's, Lt. Col. Dachar Adulyarat bullied him into touching down.

The airstrip was deserted but soon the rattle of AK-47's was heard from the surrounding jungle. Airborne again Dachar spotted a farmer not far away. He again forced the chopper pilot down and snatched him up. The farmer confirmed that the Farang, one Ernie Brace, had been captured. Bill had his ordered T-28's strafe the jungle along the runway to see if they could flush the enemy. While they were flushing F-105 Thunderchief jets appeared. Bill had not summoned them, and they were the very kind of aircraft that he didn't want for this delicate job. The Mach 2 capable 'chiefs, even at their slowest, were way too fast to be accurate. One of them couldn't even find the strip and dropped its bombs several valleys away killing innocent villagers.

The Field Marshall, who had personally ordered the useless F-105s, was unaware that Lair was permitted to order airstrikes. He immediately called the Director of Central Intelligence at Langley demanding that Lair, who he had not bothered to talk to, had never met, and who he didn't even know was the founder and head of Momentum, be reprimanded for exceeding his authority. He hadn't bothered to talk to Bill's boss Vientiane Station Chief Douglas Blaufarb either. Doug got his first word of the incident from the DCI. Upon investigation both Doug and the DCI backed Bill. No frickin' reprimand, and an extremely bad taste left in the mouths of all involved, except for the Field Marshall. In one fell swoop Bill Sullivan had made himself another big batch of enemies. It wouldn't be the last batch. The pattern was set for Sullivan's Reign in Laos. The losing combination arrogance, ego, nastiness, pigheadedness, inability to listen, inability to learn, and downright triumphal ignorance that would mark his sorry four-plus destructive years there. With Bill Sullivan around not all of Laos' *Alice in Wonderland* was homegrown.

Having experienced the full Wrath of the Field Marshall, Bill, and Momentum, did their best to "fly under the RADAR" for the remainder of 1965, while the "regulars" ramped up their bombing campaign under his micro-managerial direction and drove the USAF crazy.

The year 1966 passed quietly by Lao standards. The trends begun in '65 continued. The USAF had introduced B-52s and carpet bombing to the Trail at the tail end of '65 and expanded it immensely during the next two years. All kinds of bombing were greatly expanded with the target usually being the Trail. Since almost all the new action took place in South Laos it didn't affect Bill's operations much. The only skin he had in the South Laos game was his Lao Theung trail-watch teams. The Field Marshall was so busy pissing off the zoomies by personally selecting their targets for them that he didn't have time to meddle in Bill Lair's business. Didn't have much interest in it either. Considered it a nickel-and-dime "native" operation. Bombs and American firepower were going to win the war in Laos, and Vietnam. "Gunny" Sullivan was sure of it. Bombs and firepower and his own superb tactical skills.

On the non-bombing front the military types who had been kicked out of Laos after the signing of the Peace Accords were making a comeback, but under different names. The P.E.O. had morphed into JUSMAG (Joint US Military Assistance Group). The Green Berets and White Star Teams were gone, replaced by American advisors to new specialized RLA units christened Special Forces and Special Guerillas and Mobile Groups and Commandos. The names were different, but the game was the same. Rebuild and expand the near-useless RLA yet again while creating a bunch of "new" units that would end up being no better than the old ones. The idea was the same too. Lao units effectively led by American advisors who were ignorant of the cultures and languages of the troops they were leading. There were some American advisors who defied the stereotype and achieved success. A few RLA units became effective on the battlefield. But overall it was same old same old.

'66 produced one small RLA victory at Nam Bac 45 miles north of Luang Prabang in August. A victory that would be reversed 18 months later by a very large defeat. The annual coup was in October that year. A new twist. The RLAF instead of the RLA. The RLAF against the RLA. Their T-28's bombed RLA HQ at Chinaimo. Then their commander, General Thao Ma, flew into Wattay Airport from Thailand to claim victory. The turncoat "friendly" RLA unit that was supposed to be there to greet him had been replaced by Neutralist Commando Battalion 208 trucked in from Paksane. They executed him soon after he stepped off the plane. He was the only casualty of the coup. The RLAF operated out of Udorn Airbase. Most of its top officers were sacked and sent back to Udorn where they were kicked off the Base and also banned from Laos. Finally, in November Kong Le (1934-2014) resigned his command after being threatened by some of his officers and went into comfortable exile in France where he remained for the rest of his life.

Chapter 23: The Blond Ghost Spooks Bill Lair

The most important event of 1966 for Bill Lair and Momentum was the arrival in July of Theodore Shackley (1927-2002) as the new Vientiane Station Chief replacing Doug Blaufarb. It didn't seem important at first, but it would become of supreme importance later.

Of all the strange spooks one might meet up with in the CIA Theodore "Ted" Shackley was surely among the strangest. He was even strange looking. White blond haired, pale skinned, wraith-like, he could have been a cave-dweller or an albino. A tall slender, though somewhat bot-bellied figure, who seemed to glide noiselessly about. A secretive man who revealed little of himself. A distant, standoffish man. An intelligent man counted among the Agency's best and brightest by many. He had advanced rapidly through CIA ranks. A rumored candidate for the top spot, DCI, during the latter stages of his career.

The beginning of Shackley's career was unremarkable. Drafted right after graduating high school in 1945, he served his two years in occupied Germany. Picked up the language. Four years in college on the GI Bill preparing to be a teacher but went CIA instead. Back to Germany, Berlin, by 1952. The Ghost did well in Germany. He was made for cloak-and-dagger work, a master of deception. Smart, meticulous, connecting all the dots, silent, inobtrusive. There were few restrictions in those days, an agent could do anything he wanted to do in early postwar Germany, no such thing as legit and black ops, it was all black ops-on all sides. The kind of game silent Ted was good at...and his skill was noticed. Had a long run in Europe. His turf eventually extended to include the Soviet Union and its satellites.

Returned to the States in '59 and was assigned to Miami Station, right near his hometown of West Palm Beach. Castro had just grabbed power in Cuba and South Florida was a nest of clandestine activity the likes of postwar Berlin. Excelled again, this time in intel gathering. Turned so many Langley heads he was made Miami Station Chief in 1962 in the wake of the Bay of Pigs fiasco. Ducked the blame for that one. Escaping blame was another of Ted's strong suits. After the BOP flop a new "regime change" plan was tried out. This one designed by General Lansdale, the same guy whose theories influenced JFK to write the Kennedy Letter that allowed Bill Sullivan's self-promotion to "Field Marshall" of Laos. The Cuban version of Lansdale stressed (1) Intel gathering (2) Sabotage and propaganda (3) Free reign for the CIA to do all kinds of dirty tricks and (4) "Removal" of Fidel and his top cronies. Ted did well at #1, not so well at the other three. He was quickly 'demoted' back to Berlin in 1963 where he languished. By '63 Berlin had become a restriction-riddled backwater. No longer the happy hunting ground for spooks and spies of all stripes.

Then without warning the Lords of Langley plucked "ein Berliner" Ted from exile for Vientiane Station Chief in 1966. Many Agency insiders were surprised. None of them were more surprised than the man himself. Ted knew nothing about Laos, or Southeast Asia for that matter. Knew nothing and cared nothing. His fluency in German would be of no use there. His encyclopedic knowledge of Germany and what lurked behind the Iron Curtain ditto. Still he wasn't about to turn down a Station Chief job no matter where it was.

The man who his biographer David Corn described as "cold, calculating, almost bloodless...and weird" was coming Bill Lair's way. Soon enough Bill would be able to add a few more unflattering adjectives to that description. Nevertheless, his first impressions of "The Ghost" were positive. Shackley actively courted him at first. Took him along to some of The Field Marshall's daily charm sessions in VT. Let him speak his piece without interference. Seemed to be supporting him. Seemed to be supporting Momentum. Seemed to be fighting for the Agency against the Field Marshall. Bill wasn't afraid of the FM. Knew full well what a flaming asshole he was. Knew by now that the Agency all the way up to DCI had rallied to his defense when the FM tried to get him reprimanded. Knew that his guardian angel Des Fitzgerald still had the DCI's ear, indeed that Des was a leading candidate for DCI, and that his chance for promotion might be coming soon.

As time went by Bill began to detect the "seems to be" side of the Ghost and added 'devious' to Corn's description. He began to see that the Ghost's rather frigid chumminess was not really support, but more like picking his brain. Picking his brain and appropriating Bill's ideas as his own. Just like

"Red" Jantzen. Perhaps even more successful than felonious "Red". One of the books I delved into looking for the truth about the Secret War in Laos was written by a major player there, for a time, on the diplomatic side, who credited Ted Shackley for the success of Momentum. He even credited Ted with being the founder and genius behind Momentum. I wonder where he got that info? I'm not going to tell you his name or the title of his book. He doesn't really figure in Bill Lairs' bio. Apparently didn't even know Bill existed as he makes no reference to him in his book. A clean sweep for the elusive Ghost. Certainly, self-promotion was one of his skills. Perhaps his greatest skill.

Bill also found that 'devious' was a good word to use as it applied to the Ghost's covert attempt to get rid of his indispensable righthand man Pat Landry. He never knew just why the Ghost wanted to can Pat. To be sure Pat was an acquired taste and the Ghost was as much his opposite as anyone living. Perhaps the Ghost decided that he only needed one brain to pick to acquire his mastery of Momentum and decided it should be Bill. Which didn't augur well for Bill's future either as once the Ghost was master of Momentum details, he could rid himself of Bill too. The Ghost's attempted hatchet job was quickly detected by both Bill and its intended victim. Neither quiet countrified Bill nor brash foul-mouthed Pat were men to be trifled with. The Ghost sent his man Tom Clines (1928-2013) to understudy Pat who immediately smelled a rat; isolated him from the most critical things he was doing and set him to counting beans and churning out low priority reports. The burly voluble Clines, as much the opposite of his boss as Pat was of his, didn't take offense and, over time, became more supportive of Bill and Pat than he was of his boss.

Chapter 24: The Dynamic Duo and the Supermarket War

With the Ghost thwarted and Pat Landry still sloppily at his desk bellowing obscenities and slapping his swagger stick for emphasis Momentum was back to normal. But it was a new normal now. The Udorn Airbase was exploding with the speed of Bloody Borger from the ghost town it had been when the Bill and Pat show first arrived. Udorn had just brought in a gusher of money. Low budget seat-of-the-pants Momentum was in danger of being swept away in a flood of cash. Now no operation was too unsuccessful to avoid being showered with bucks. No idea so crackpot as to avoid lavish funding. The Ghost himself got it right when he dubbed it "The Supermarket War", and also correct when he described the Bill and Pat Show as "The Country Store War". Hangars now lined the once grassy edges of the runways. Buildings were springing up everywhere. The base was one vast construction zone. Hundreds of aircraft and the thousands of men needed to fly and maintain them were pouring in. Ugly Udorn was getting even uglier, and bigger. All manner of shacks and lean-tos and hovels constructed of bamboo, rattan, dismembered packing crates, retired parachutes, steel runway panels from the early temp runway that had been replaced with permanent cement, Styrofoam and plastic bomb packing, and flattened out beer cans were spreading over the rice fields surrounding the town. The best paying job for Thais was "guh-lee"(prostitute). The hottest growth industry commercial sex. Next hottest treating VD. Next after that selling beer and pot.

All this harried activity was to support the Vietnam War, not the Secret War in Laos. Except for the area of South Laos occupied by the Ho Chi Minh Trail it was business as usual in Laos. But it wouldn't be business as usual for long. Momentum HQ was still in building AP1 its old familiar digs looking even shabbier now amidst the booming construction. A prime candidate to be torn down and replaced with something bigger and better. In August of 1966 a zoomie Captain named Richard Secord (1932-) was picking his way through the tangle trying to find an outfit called the 4802nd something or other. Nobody seemed to know where it was. Most were probably too new to know where anything was. He had been assigned as the USAF Liaison to this unit, whatever it was. Fresh from mid-career training at age 34 he hoped it would be something good. Secord had already had a wild and exciting career in the

Air Force. Had flown 200 missions in Vietnam in a T-28 in the guise of a South Vietnamese pilot during 1962 and 63 when the US wasn't supposed to have any combatants in the Republic. Done much the same thing in the Shah of Iran's air force. He was used to strange places and strange duties. He was in for another one as soon as he found AP1.

Once he found the 4802nd he quickly realized that it was even stranger than any place the Air Force had sent him before. One look at pot-bellied Pat Landry in shorts and flip-flops said it all. Nobody knew he was coming. The spare quiet guy with the thick glasses who sat with his desk facing that of the fat noisy guy asked him if Ted Shackley had sent him. He didn't know who Ted Shackley was. Maybe he was in the wrong place with his spotless uniform and stiff West Point military manner. The diffident guy with the glasses gave him a short briefing on the Secret War in Laos. That we were running it under a false front of neutrality. That our Ambassador was telling the USAF where to bomb and trying to tell everyone else what to do. That the only effective fighting force in the Kingdom was some mountain tribe. A little taste of *Alice*. Then the quiet guy, who he by this time had found out was Bill Lair, told him to go see Laos for himself and come back in a month or so when it stopped raining. So much for Momentum Orientation.

Captain Secord did as he was ordered. Did a good job of it too, as he did of everything he was ordered to do. He was good at working on his own in exotic locales. Visited all the hot spots. Met all the players. Sorted out all the confusing varieties of friendly and enemy forces. Soaked up more understanding of the Secret War in a few weeks than many of the Americans who'd been there for years. Came to understand what few Americans other than Bill Lair and Pat Landry did. That the war in Laos was the flip side of the war in Vietnam. That in South Vietnam the US and ARVN troops were in "injun country"; constantly being harassed, ambushed, hit-and-runned, booby-trapped and bombarded by the NVA and Vietcong. Forced to stick close to the roads. Forced to fortify their bases. That the bulk of their fighting men were tied down in support and defense. In Laos, at least in Hmong Country, things were exactly the opposite. The PL and NVA were in "injun country" having the same problems as our troops had in Vietnam. And it was Bill Lair's odd, offbeat, low-budget operation that kept them there.

Dick Secord came to have great respect for Bill Lair and Pat Landry even though his USAF and their Momentum were totally opposite in the way they fought the Secret War. Called them "real artists at moving people around, at drawing blood from the enemy". Called them "cool, calm and reasoned...in command of every situation they faced". Said they had great chemistry; nicknamed them "The Dynamic Duo".

"I learned more in my first year in Laos than I'd learned in the previous ten years". Was Dick's final assessment.

He had little to do with Ted Shackley while he was liaison to the 4802nd. Later, in a new role, he'd meet the Ghost and learn to hate him, or in his exact words "I didn't particularly care for the bastard" and conclude that "Ted didn't know shit about tactics". Maybe that was the Ghost's secret. He only seemed to know about tactics. Bill would also later conclude that "Ted didn't know shit..." about some other things as well.

In the meantime, Bill and Pat continued their fight to save the Hmong and keep Momentum from being drowned in a sea of cash. Soon ratty old Ap1 would be history. By mid-1967 it was replaced by a spiffy new state-of-the-art HQ populated by an ever-growing army of what Bill dreaded most. Secretaries! Udorn bachelor Bill was in danger of being overrun by a platoon of bored USAF officers' wives looking for something to do and some extra income. But it could have been worse. He wouldn't have had anything for them to do if the Field Marshall hadn't commanded Momentum account for every bag of rice and round of ammo airlifted to Hmong Country and the dates, times and places it was sent. Plus, a raft of daily activity reports the equivalent of *War and Peace* to be deposited on his VT Embassy desk each morning. In addition to his Secretary Corps he had so many new agents he didn't know what to do with them all, though he had plenty of offices for them in the new HQ which he sarcastically dubbed "The Taj Mahal".

Bill Lair and Momentum had survived the first half of 1967 intact as had Vang Pao and the Hmong. The same old things happened in Hmong Country. The PDJ changed hands once again. The Hmong's hit-and-run guerilla war continued supplemented by piston-pounder air support. Pop Buell had his ever-growing refugee camp now relocated to Sam Thong five miles and two ridges away from VP's Long Cheng HQ functioning smoothly. Things were settled enough there that he could indulge in a bit of the agronomy work he'd been sent to do in Laos by the IVS seven years before but hadn't had the time for. His crop substitution for opium seemed promising. Sweet potatoes and garlic looked like they could be winners. Unfortunately, the composting of human and animal manure which the Hmong had a taboo against, but which had now become necessary for the public health of the crowded refugee camps, had a bad side effect. The composted shit made Hmong gardens bloom with tomatoes the size of soft balls...and increased opium poppy yields enormously as well. Poppies hadn't been included in Pop's experiments, but the Hmong had test plots of their own.

The biggest threat to Bill's six months of the status quo was the Ghost's insistence that he, and VP, provide more Hmong troops to send south where they were being used as mercenaries to fight Uncle Sam's Supermarket war to obliterate the Ho Chi Minh Trail; an operation that was making no headway whatsoever in spite of its ever-increasing tonnage of bombs ,mines, motion dectectors, napalm, and Agent Orange. VP was not so desperate that he needed to recruit boy soldiers yet, but he, and Bill, could see that things were headed in that direction. Hmong casualties had been modest to this point, but more young men had to be recruited to fill the slots of those veteran fighters being sucked into the maw of the US's conventional war down South.

Things began to look darker as the second half of '67 arrived. On July 23, 1967 Bill's guardian angel Des Fitzgerald dropped dead of a heart attack at the age of 57 in the middle of a tennis match. From then on Bill, and Momentum, would be working without a net. They would have no one to cover their backs in Washington. But that was a possible future problem. A clear and present danger, not just to Bill and Momentum, but to the whole US effort in Laos was looming.

Chapter 25: The Armchair Military Strategists Run Amok

In July of 1967 what might be called an extended "Amateur Night" for wannabee Napoleons began. Legitimate military minds like those of Bill Lair and Pat Landry and young Dick Secord were either ignored or overridden. It was time for the back-seat-driving chessboard crew to make their brilliant moves. The result was a dog's breakfast of knuckleheaded maneuvers not seen since the Civil War days of the "Young Napoleon" General George McClellan's Peninsular Campaign. They started with Nam Bac, an inconsequential village 50 roadless miles northwest of Luang Prabang and 45 miles from the border of North Vietnam, 30 of which were traversed by Route 19. Set in a ridge-rimmed valley that was yet another near-perfect replica of Dienbienphu.

Nam Bac had already changed hands several times since 1960. The RLA "captured" it in a much-hyped victory in 1966. "Captured" is in quotes as it is unclear if the enemy, a couple of ratty understrength PL battalions, stuck around long enough to defend it. By August '67 the men of the NVA's crack veteran 316th Division came to take it back. They didn't have far to come and only 15 miles of it would be on foot. The brass of the RLA's General Staff convinced themselves that if they did grab it, it would be "next stop Luang Prabang". That threat was more imaginary than real. If seizing LP was the NVA's intent, there was a much better path to follow. They could easily retake the junction of Routes 7 and 13 at Sala Phou Khoun which they had recently held and cruise 50 miles up Route 13 to the gates of LP.

And as for their intent, there was no logical reason to believe that Hanoi wanted to take LP. The Geneva Accords of '62 had rather fuzzily partitioned Laos into Communist, Neutralist and Royalist zones as per Bill Sullivan's earlier plan. It also listed the major cities and towns in each zone. The NVA had encroached on the boundaries of the Royalist and Neutralist zones but had never taken any of their towns or cities. The Field Marshall wasn't the only one maintaining the fantasy of the Accords. Hanoi was maintaining parts of it too. Especially the part in which they declared that they had no troops in

Laos. It was easy to protect that fiction if all their troops remained in the jungle, much harder if some of them were swaggering around the streets of Luang Prabang. In addition, they were supposedly committed to the fiction of supporting Buddhism and the Monarchy. The capture of LP would make that a very public lie. In fact, LP would be one of the last Royalist cities occupied by the Communists when they finally seized power in 1975. It was never really threatened until then.

A sketchy half-baked battle plan with a dubious rationale behind it. But it didn't have to happen. It wouldn't happen unless the US footed the bill for the RLA's grandiose offensive. Footed the bill, airlifted the 7,500 proposed troops into the "valley of death", provided all the weapons and supplies and logistical support, provided most of the air support. The US had veto power over the whole sorry misbegotten, potentially disastrous, mess. The Ghost came to Bill Lair for advice…or maybe just to cover his ass in case the project went sour. He probably didn't like what Bill told him though it was hard to say as he maintained his usual Sphinx-like reserve upon hearing the "bad news".

Bill delivered his advice in his usual calm, clear, deliberate manner. Should the Agency back the RLA's Nam Bac Plan? Answer "No". Why not? Answer (1) The only way to supply the huge liberation force would be by air. The single small airstrip would be in NVA artillery range as soon as they surrounded the valley. In range of their direct fire weapons as soon as they took the ridges overlooking the valley. (2) Even if they got supplies the RLA's logistical abilities were nil. Bill had been an eyewitness to that at Phoumi's "Battle of Vientiane"; and they were no better now than they had been then despite the hundreds of thousands of hours of training and tens of millions of dollars poured into them by the US since. (3) The RLA's "command structure" was a joke. Most of its officers, especially the highest-ranking ones, were either incompetent or corrupt or both, usually both. They got their jobs by bloodline not ability. (4) Despite all the new "Groupments Mobile (GMs)" JUSMAG had created in an attempt turn the RLA into an offensive powerhouse the thing it still did best (if want to call it 'best') was to sit on its ass and wait for artillery and air support; which was another thing that hadn't changed since Phoumi's great 1960 Vientiane Victory. Nam Bac Valley would provide the perfect setting for the RLA to play its inertial strong suit. (5) The terrain was unfavorable…on steroids. Nam Bac Valley was Mother Nature's equivalent of the La Brea tarpits for armies.

The Ghost took Bill Lair's very specific and passionate advice and blew off the lot of it. Why the CIA's fair haired fast tracked "genius" did such an abysmally stupid thing is hard to say. Several arguments were made for it, none of them by Bill. The strongest of them is that the Ghost, despite his seemingly firm stand for the Agency and against the Field Marshall, was secretly scared to death of him, or rather was scared to death that he would use his high-placed connections in Washington to wreck the Ghost's CIA career, which was a distinct possibility. The FM's "summary executions" of anyone in his organization who dared oppose him, and his straight-to-top-without-checking-the-facts attack on Bill Lair in the case of his attempted rescue of Ernie Brace had rattled the outwardly cool Ghost. Sullivan was gung-ho for Operation Prasane as it was christened. A sentiment he would later deny, among other things, many other things. By his actions the Ghost seemed determined to out gung-ho him. He even went the FM one step further in folly by preparing a position paper titled "US Policy in Northern Laos" which proposed "a defensive line running west to east from Muong Sing to Muong Sai to Nam Bac to Phou Pha Thi" to protect Luang Prabang and "prevent Communist expansion." A Maginot Line in triple canopy jungle? A recycled Belgian defensive plan from WWI? What sort of a line? Bunkers? Pillboxes? 12-inch naval guns? The Ghost's plan went beyond merely moronic to insane. Since he proudly copied his plan to Langley and elsewhere it was hard to deny it later. But the nuttiest part of his proposal was saved for last. Once his 'line' had been established the Ghost cautioned that the friendlies "should refrain from actions which could provoke serious enemy retaliation". "Serious retaliation"? NVA commanders would be too busy laughing their asses off! Build a great wall defensive line and then be careful not to disturb the enemy? The Ghost's hallucinatory blueprint never was implemented. Luckily, though not for him, the "Battle of Nam Bac II" was over before it could be seriously considered.

On 18 July 1967 the battle officially began. American choppers lifted the first RLA troops into Nam Bac valley (which they had negligently abandoned after their 1966 "victory") where they defeated the Communist enemy. Or maybe they didn't defeat them as no casualties were reported and there may have been no resistance. Nevertheless, they declared a great Victory, just as they had the year before. Soon NVA troops would be getting off trucks at the dead-end of Route 19 and setting out to cover the final 15 miles to Nam Bac on foot. Over the coming weeks Air America would pour the rest of the scheduled 4,500 RLA troops into the valley while the NVA was surrounding it, roughing in their underground bunkers and supply trail network, and setting up their artillery firebases. The Ghost demanded that Vang Pao's "Meo irregulars", as he insisted on calling them, join the fight; which they did by staging hit and run diversionary attacks from three Hmong villages just north of Nam Bac. Roughly a thousand Hmong troops were involved. As of September, they were the only ones who'd done any real fighting. The RLA did their usual thing. Sat in their defensive works burrowing ever deeper. The six battalions of elite Groupments Mobile (GM)s were busy digging shoulder to with the RLA regulars. The airstrip was soon shelled out of commission and supplies, and any reinforcements, would have to be dropped in. Food would soon begin to get short. The command structure would fall apart. Everything Bill told the Ghost was going to become true. Several other things he didn't tell him would also become true. As there was no reliable communication between RLAF T-28 bombers and ground troops most of the RLA casualties would be caused by friendly bombs. The RLA commander Prince General Bounchanh would order the RLAF to quit bombing. Fast-moving USAF jets from Udorn would fly sorties and miss their targets as badly as the RLAF had. Friendly artillery support from the mass of US Howitzers, recoilless rifles and mortars in the valley would be described as "non-existent to awful".

In November the Field Marshall, seconded by the Ghost, ordered up Thai Troops to save the day. By that time the only way any large number of troops could get to Nam Bac was overland, so only a few of them showed, choppered in by gutsy Air America pilots. Only a handful of Thais so the FM and the Ghost demanded Bill Lair send more Hmong, at least 2,000 of them. He was reluctant to send them. So was Vang Pao. But what could either of them do? They set off through the jungle from the outskirts of Luang Prabang. Maybe Bill and VP told them to take their time about it, maybe not. Both the Field Marshall and the Ghost later would say they did, but they were anything but what could be called "reliable sources". It wouldn't have been a fast trip even if Bill and VP had been enthusiastic; and their reinforcements would find the NVA blocking their path for the final stretch of it. The Siege of Nam Bac dragged on for the rest of 1967. By the first week of '68 it had reached its last gasp. On 11 January the NVA, who had done little offensively to that point beyond bombarding the Valley, stepped up their attack. Stepped it up so much that Prince General Bounchanh fled by chopper deserting his own troops to save his royal ass. Shortly thereafter everything that hadn't already collapsed, collapsed.

The "after action" report of the Nam Bac fiasco was shocking, but not because of the high number of casualties. That number was hazy, but surprisingly low. Best guess? 100 RLA and 100 Hmong dead, that included any RLA troops who were seriously wounded as the RLA had no functional Medical Corps. The Hmong had PARU medics, so their wounded had a better chance of survival. The total of weapons lost was much more specific. Basically, all the ordnance that had been sent, was lost. Including 7 US Howitzers, 49 recoilless rifles, 52 mortars, and enough M-1 rifles and carbines to equip 4,000 or so troops. When the RLA mustered the "Defenders of Nam Bac" after the battle they could count only as far as 1,400 (of 4,500). And the rest? 100 probably dead, 600 or so captured, and the biggie-2400 deserted and changed sides. And don't forget six (of the eleven) GMs that JUSMAG had so expensively trained and equipped disappeared and never to be seen or heard from again. The whole ghastly production brought to you by the King of the Micromanagers Ambassador William H. Sullivan and his faithful lackey and master planner CIA Station Chief Theodore "The Man with the Photographic Memory" Shackley. It was enough to make even the Ghost's "hit man" Tom Clines desert him and change sides. It was enough to make Bill Lair sick, and he'd become even sicker in the future when the Field Marshall and the Ghost tried to blame him for their disaster.

Chapter 26: Out of the Frying Pan and into the Line of Fire

The dust from Nam Bac had not even begun to settle when a second very different kind of disaster loomed. It had begun at about the same time as Operation Prasane and was playing out on roughly the same timetable. The location of this building fiasco was Phou (mountain) Pha Thi. The same place that would have been the anchor of the Ghost's imaginative and imaginary Maginot Line.

By mid-1967 the Ho Chi Minh Trail had become the only game in town for Washington policymakers. Nothing else in Laos mattered. They had thrown everything they could think of at the Trail. Bombs of course, tens of thousands of tons of them. More than had been thrown against Nazi Germany in WWII. Dick Secord, now a Major, was tasked with finding targets for them all but Field Marshall Sullivan made up his own list at his US Embassy desk and forced it down Dick's throat. What that had to do with Diplomacy God only knows. Napalm, Agent Orange, anti-personnel mines, movement detectors; the corridor which the Trail passed through was blasted, beaten up, ploughed up, defoliated, scorched, mined and poisoned but the trucks kept rolling. Special Guerrilla Units and Lao Theung trail-watchers and RLA Special Forces Battalions were thrown at it from the Lao side. Montagnard "irregulars" and US Special Forces and Green Berets and Vietnamese equivalents of Lao SGUs were thrown at it from the South Vietnam side. That great military visionary Secretary of Defense Robert McNamara even proposed building a high-tech fence across the Trail. A fence accompanied by a state-of-the-art grab-bag of technical wonders including a range of sensors and night vision devices. There was even a rainmaking plan to drown the enemy out. This was good old American ingenuity at its best. Only one problem. Most of Mac's Wizard War stuff either didn't work at all in the field or didn't work well enough to matter. And still the trucks kept rolling. The more hurt the US laid on the Trail the more supplies and men it delivered. A study by the Rand Corporation (remember their Omega game?) reported that 10% of the supplies sent down the Trail were being destroyed. So what? The Soviet Union had a near-bottomless inventory of WWII surplus. No wonder they quit Laos. They were destroying their Capitalist enemy in

Southeast Asia on the cheap without risking anything. The results of the Omega game were coming true. Even Dick Secord, the Air Force's man in charge of targeting, knew that bombing, and all the other stuff, wasn't working. The only way to shut down the Trail was with boots on the ground. American boots. But that could be done only over Bill Sullivan's dead body. American boots on the ground in Laos, real boots not sheep-dipped boots and disguised boots, would wreck his (and the Crocodile's) masterwork, the Geneva Accords of 1962.

But Mac's wizards had yet another high-tech wonder to try out. Maybe this one would do the trick. Bill Lair didn't know about this new one until he was "invited" to the Base HQ of the 7/13th Air Force at Udorn. When he got there, he was in for a shock.

****

Author's note: The 7/13th, was a bizarre amalgam of the 7th AF which was HQ'd in Saigon and the 13th AF which was HQ'd at Clark AFB in the Philippines. A tangled creation that proved to be a chain-of-command nightmare. The Vietnam War produced a lot of awkward barely functional such beasts. Like my outfit. The 7th RRFS was located at Ramasun Station, but its HQ was 300 miles away in Bangkok at Mekala Station which was also the home of the 83rd RRSOU which I was assigned to for my first nine months at Ramasun. Oh, and our payroll office was 200 miles away in Korat. The Colonel who commanded this combined unit rarely visited us at Ramasun, which is where 90% of his troops were stationed.

Bill was greeted at the 7/13th by a team of the brassiest of Brass headed by a four-star General who was the Commander-in-Chief of the Pacific Air Command and had his HQ in Hawaii. 4-star Generals rarely found their way to the wilds of Udorn, nor did the entourage of lesser Generals and Colonels who accompanied him. Bill was acting as a stand-in for his boss, The Ghost, who said he had "a scheduling conflict". A four-star General complete with lackeys comes to meet him in Udorn and he's too busy to see them? That has a certain odd aroma about it. Perhaps another indication of the gutless coward lurking behind The Ghost's cool commanding façade.

The big cheese, ably assisted by his followers, proceeded to brief the low-level 'field man' Bill Lair on the workings of a fresh new piece of wizard war equipment. Two Generals and three full bird Colonels briefing the civilian equivalent of a Lt. Colonel? Bet that didn't happen often, if ever, during the Vietnam War. Bill may have been wondering "why me?" until the Briefing Team got to the point of mentioning exactly what the new equipment did and where they proposed to put it. Pha Thi Mountain aka Lima site 85. A place Bill Lair knew only too well. To the Hmong it was their most sacred mountain. It had defied Vietnamese conquest since before there was a Ho Chi Minh or a Democratic Republic of Vietnam. It was the last refuge of the Sam Neua Hmong in hard times...and a finger thrust squarely into the eye of Hanoi, which was only a hundred and fifty air miles away. Take one look at it and you'd know why.

Not the highest peak in Laos but the weirdest. It was easy to see why the Hmong could think that their dead ancestors and gods dwelt there. An enormous sheer-sided limestone monolith. Three faces of it so steep as to be considered unscalable. The fourth only barely scalable. Riddled with caves large and small as are all limestone peaks. Even the top of the mountain had only a few tiny flat spots. It was narrow and craggy with so little habitable space that the Hmong village which clung precariously to it numbered not much above a hundred souls. Three or four companies of Hmong soldiers (3-400 men) had been enough to defend it against NVA attacks. Most of them were positioned at the foot of the mountain on the barely scalable east side next to the L-85 airstrip. The Agency had tried to establish a Helio strip up top, but it was so dangerous that, after a couple of near-suicidal landings and takeoffs, they abandoned it. Other than its spiritual value Pha Thi was worthless, except for a small patch of the sweetest poppy growing ground in all of Hmong Country.

But the USAF thought that a chunk of Pha Thi's precarious mountaintop real estate was highly desirable. They had established a tiny helipad and a navigational beacon called a TACAN there in '66 with Bill Lair's blessing. He even told them where to put it. 6000 feet above sea level and by USAF standards only a stone's throw from Hanoi it was the perfect place for it. The top of Pha Thi had such a stupendous view he thought it might make a nice spot for a vacation cabin. The new piece of USAF electronic wizardry was called the Model TSQ-81 and the zoomies called its installation and operation Commando Club. The "81" would support equipment recently installed aboard their bombers that would allow "blind bombing". A sort of combined autopilot and auto-bomber. Bombers would almost fly themselves to the target and drop their loads without human intervention. Rain or shine, you didn't even have to see your target to hit it with pin-point accuracy. Flying a bombing sortie against the enemy would from now on be no more demanding than driving a bus, and probably safer.

****

Author's note: The oft-uttered incantation "pin-point accuracy" as used by the USAF was always a rather dodgy proposition. In practice it seemed to range from "able to hit a barn door with a steam shovel" at best to "somewhere in the same general vicinity" at worst. That averaged out to a "pin-point" the size of a football field. Which was the accuracy USAF bombers would attain once during the Battle of Pha Thi when they attacked an NVA warehouse clearly visible to spotters atop the mountain. Bombs rained down and when the smoke cleared the warehouse was still standing, but a football field sized area of jungle surrounding it was cleanly levelled.

****

Digital ground support for auto-bombing would require more equipment atop Pha Thi. Equipment that would need much more human care and feeding than what was there now. The new gear was all pre-packaged and ready to go. At some point the 4-star and his Briefing Team stopped for questions. Bill hadn't asked any so far. Hadn't said anything so far. Had sat quietly with his eyes averted. Since Ted Shackley's arrival the naturally reticent Lair had become even more close-mouthed. The Air Force Team had to ask him what he thought before he uttered so much as a single syllable. The brass had done their homework. They knew who Bill Lair was. Knew that he knew more than any other CIA man, or any other man period, about Laos. They knew that he'd given the USAF his blessing the year before. They wanted his blessing again for their new improved project. Finally, the Oracle of Laos spoke in his customary humble slow deliberate manner.

"Yeah, you can put the new equipment on the mountain. It will last a while. But Hanoi will find out about it, and once they've found out about it, they'll start planning to destroy it..."

He went on to detail his take on Pha Thi in a much more deliberate manner than they had theirs, but with as much chapter and verse. The early warning sign that Hanoi's plan was operational would be the construction of roads and trails from the border of North Vietnam, which was barely ten air miles away. The Communists were creatures of habit. They always did the same things, in the same order, when they set out on a major offensive. Built their 'infrastructure' first. Their roads, their bomb-proof bunkers, their bomb-proof supply depots, their well-protected firebases...zeroed-in their howitzers and mortars. Then it would be time for the Commando Club boys to start leaning toward the door, but still some time left. Once their infrastructure was in place, they'd send their shock troops, as many as they thought they needed with more held in reserve in case things didn't go according to plan. That would be the time for the friendlies to fold their tents and steal away into the night taking their pre-packaged gear with them. Steal away and set up on another mountaintop, a mountaintop not as good as Pha Thi, which was the best in Laos, but good enough. And if the NVA wanted to grab that one they'd have to start their predictable plan all over again. Pure Bill Lair philosophy. Lots of high mountains in Laos. If one outpost is threated move to another and keep on truckin'. Don't try to go head to head with the NVA at the thing they're best at.

And another thing. Don't expect that Hmong troops will be able to defend Pha Thi. They won't. And don't expect that American air power will be able to defend it either. It won't by itself. If you want to defend Pha Thi you'll need American troops, elite Airborne troops...and air support. Do you really want to do all that when you could pull out and pitch your tents somewhere else in a matter of days? The Air Force men left the meeting excited about Commando Club. Bill Lair, and Major Dick Secord, who also attended but said even less than he did, left confused. How could they still be so upbeat after Bill's downbeat assessment of Pha Thi's security situation? Did they buy his "take a powder when Pha Thi is threatened" line? Dick the Air Force guy thought not. That didn't fit the USAF way of doing things. Bill was worried too. The NVA was already at work trying to reverse the Hmong near-takeover of Sam Neua Province. Commando Club was sure to bring a flood of new NVA into the area. If the Field Marshall had been in on the Udorn confab he would have bristled with anger at Bill's contention that the only way Pha Thi could be defended was with American boots on the ground in Laos. Were all the American players going to be on the same page for the Model TSQ-81 upgrade? Not bloody likely!

Chapter 27: A Few Choice Words From LBJ

Not everyone in Thailand and Laos was on the same page but that didn't make any difference. A cable from President Lyndon Baines Johnson to Ambassador William Sullivan said, "Do it!" and it was done. Commando Club became reality on July 1, 1967, regardless of the consequences, either foreseen or un-foreseen. A few weeks later an obviously military man who seemed uncomfortable in civvies arrived at Vientiane Station to see Ted Shackley who was, once again, "too busy" to meet with him. Another bad move, Ghost, you just brushed off the sheep-dipped USAF Colonel who's in charge of Commando Club. Snubbed by the CIA the "don't-call-me Colonel" went to the Embassy and met with the Air Attaché instead. The Attaché took him to meet with Ambassador Sullivan. The three of them quickly agreed that Pha Thi was a potentially dangerous place and that the Commando Club staff would be given plenty of time to escape if attack threatened. It took longer for Sullivan to lead the Colonel (whoops!) through the byzantine procedures that would protect them against being spotted as US Military personnel, even though it would take no more than one look at any of them to see that that was exactly what they were. All Commando Club personnel would be covered with a thick coating of false identification as CIVILIAN employees of Lockheed Aircraft Services including the requisite ID cards and fake passports and supporting documentation. A thorough sheep-dipping.

Opening ceremonies complete. Lt. Colonel Gerald Clayton (sorry 'bout that…what was his name supposed to be again?) and his ALL CIVILIAN crew fell to the task of getting the Model TSQ-81 up and running. Some of the USAF's biggest cargo choppers lifted it from Udorn to Pha Thi in pieces depositing it near the edge of a sheer limestone cliff next to the existing TACAN site like a bunch of house trailers. A new Radar dish was installed atop the old TACAN building. The contents of the "house trailers" were unpacked and installed complete with a system that would blow the whole damned facility straight to Hell if need be to keep its cutting-edge technology from being captured by the enemy. Placed at the highest point on southernmost end the mountaintop the operational site was so small that there wasn't room for anything else. The old runway, which had been converted into a helipad, was some distance north of it down a single steep narrow path. Next to it was a knot of small buildings which the Commando Club boys enlarged to accommodate the extra staff that would be needed to operate the new system. The two CIA agents atop PT bunked with them but spent most of their time with Hmong troops and Thai PARU who were at the other end of the mountaintop along with the Hmong villagers. Trenches were dug, mines laid, a bunker was established next to the barracks, explosive bobby traps were planted-sure footed Hmong rappelling down all four sides of the mountain to set them, trip wires were strung. But the mountaintop was so narrow and rocky that there wasn't room for much in the way of defensive works and clear fields of fire were limited. The inherent claustrophobic dangers of Pha Thi were apparent. But what the hell, the NVA wouldn't make it to PT anyway, and even if they did make it to the foot of the mountain, they'd never reach the top. This was an all Air Force show (despite the silly-ass civilian cover) and the enemy would be bombed into oblivion.

The installation went along with the usual USAF efficiency. Only one small glitch. A pair of visiting Buddhist monks appeared on 20 October to take pictures and make sketches. Visiting Buddhist monks atop the sacred mountain of the Animist Hmong? Monks with cameras? Monks with sketch pads? Something's wrong here. The "monks" and their cameras and their sketch pads were quickly choppered off to Long Cheng and never seen again. VP knew how to treat his Vietnamese enemies. Torture them first, then kill 'em. The Hmong hadn't survived centuries of conflict with the Viets by showing them mercy. If this lame attempt at spying was indicative of the enemy's clandestine genius, then there was at least one thing the friendlies didn't have to fear from them.

Comic relief? Not quite. Bill Lair knew what the 'fake monks' incident meant. It meant that the Viets were already at work on their plan for Pha Thi even before the TSQ-81 was up and running. Their countdown had already begun. The USAF's lease on Pha Thi might be even shorter that he thought it would be. And now that he knew that Commando Club was being done specifically by Presidential order, he doubted that his "steal away" plan would be implemented. Who would be the guy who'd tell LBJ "Sorry, Mr. President, we gotta' get outta' Pha Thi, things are gettin' too hot for us."

Bill saw a lot of things not to like at Pha Thi, especially on top of it. The defensive forces were strung out along the top. It was difficult for them to keep in touch with each other or with the troops in the valley below. The American Commando Club staff isolated themselves from the "native troops" in their barracks. Bill always insisted that any Americans working for him hang with the locals for their own protection and to keep up on the most immediate intel. None of the 15-20 Americans at the TACAN site spoke Lao. Bill's American agents and Thai PARU could have interpreted for them and defended them if their site came under attack. But they kept to themselves, which meant that if crunch time came, they'd have only themselves for defense. A bunch of communications techies who were barred by the Field Marshall from having weapons. What kind of a defense could they make?

****

Author's note: I can tell you what kind of a defense that would be. It might not be quite as pathetic a defense as the lingies and traffic analysts and radio-heads of Ramasun Station would have made if we'd been attacked, which, thank God, we never were. The techies atop Pha Thi were perhaps more military than we were. Perhaps, though half of the troops at Ramasun were zoomies who had the same skill sets as those atop Pha Thi. And the Field Marshall's defensive plan for PT was even more ludicrous than Ramasun's.

****

By the time Commando Club was up and running in early November Bill Lair and Ted Shackley were wary of each other. Bill's confidence in Ted's ability and intelligence had vanished. Sure, he had some good points. He paid more attention to his Agency troops in the field than any of his predecessors had. He consulted regularly with Bill, which is something those same predecessors had done only sporadically, or not at all. Even though he was systematically replacing Bill's Laos veterans with his own mostly rookies he was doing it honestly and openly. But the real source of Bill's anger was that Ted was running the Secret War in Laos all wrong. He consulted with Bill, seemed to be listening, then proceeded to do exactly what Bill had not recommended. He was a good enough human being, but willfully ignorant of all things Laos, and just plain full of shit. Shit that had already hit the fan at Nam Bac. Shit that could hit the fan at Pha Thi. Maybe it was just his wounded pride. Why had his old mentor, Des Fitzgerald, picked the Ghost as VT Station Chief, and not him? Alas it was too late to ask that question now. Des was dead, and Bill was stuck with Ted.

Chapter 28: High Times atop Pha Thi Mountain

The year of 1967 was near its end and everything was humming nicely on top of Pha Thi Mountain and in the valley below. Or so it seemed. The new '81' system worked slick, even though most USAF bomber crews hated it and refused use it. During November and December, they only used it on one-sixth of their sorties. Who wants to be demoted to airborne bus driver? But there was no doubt that, when they used it, it worked. The AF may not have made believers out of their own flight crews but folks in Hanoi were sold on it and determined to get rid of it. Since they were the ones under those Commando Club guided bombs, they were more closely acquainted with them than the men who delivered them. Three NVA battalions had come into Laos in early November to clear Vang Pao's Hmong outposts so they could improve and supplement the roads to Pha Thi. By mid-December they were probing PT's outer defenses; skirmishing with VP's village militias a few miles east of the mountain. The Hmong were operating as usual, melting away when strongly attacked, then returning when the NVA moved on. In Udorn Bill and Pat marked the spot of each small clash. The pattern was clear. The marks were clustered like bees on the scale-able east face of the mountain. Both sides were operating as usual. Bill passed the regular stream of detailed intel to the Ghost and his USAF liaison Dick Secord. Dick kept the USAF photo interpreters at Udorn searching for the building ganglion of new roads and trails, but sometimes he couldn't find enough targets to keep his bombers busy. They were just too well hidden. Other times he found targets and couldn't get planes to bomb them. The Air Force was becoming rather nonchalant about the defense of Pha Thi; and its tangled chain of command didn't help, especially when he requested assistance from Saigon. They had their own war to fight and Laos was low priority.

On January 12, 1968 a strange incident occurred that could be viewed either as more comic relief or a portent of bad things to come. The North Vietnamese Air Force entered the fray in Laos. To be sure Hanoi did have an Air Force, a hundred or so obsolescent Soviet Migs and well-trained pilots to fly them. An Air Force that had acquitted itself nobly during the early years of the Vietnam War and shot down a good number of USAF fighters. But that Air Force had been withdrawn to Kunming China in 1966 due to heavy losses. Its planes could be easily replaced, more Soviet war surplus-Korea this time, but it's pilots couldn't. We at Ramasun Station kept an eye on them. They still hadn't moved as of 1971. However, part of Hanoi's AF had been left behind. It was easy to see why it had been left behind.

The Antonov AN-2 is one of the ugliest airplanes ever to take to the skies. A cloth-covered bi-plane that looks like an overgrown version of something out of WWI but was still in production in 1967. Used as a crop duster and STOL bush plane, it was not made to fight and didn't look as if it could be made to fight. But fight it did...at least one time, in Laos. More Laos *Alice in Wonderland* you might say. Four AN-2's flying in neat formation were spotted southeast of Sam Neua town on a fateful day in January. Two peeled away but the other two chugged slowly toward Pha Thi belching greasy black exhaust as they made three passes over the mountain dropping bombs (actually mortar shells) through holes cut in their floors, firing machine guns, and shooting shoulder-fired B-40 rockets (the equivalent of a bazooka) through their open side doors. Most of their fire was concentrated on the tin-roofed CIA building near the helipad. One B-40 rocket was fired at the TACAN site and missed. They also strafed the Hmong village killing two women and wounding two men. One of the CIA officers on the ground shot at them with an M-16 and claimed he hit a Colt (the name given to the AN-2 by *Janes' Fighting Aircraft*). One of the two bombers crashed and burned on the west side of the mountain. An Air America chopper was on the helipad at the time of the attack. The Colts managed not to hit it, so it took off and chased after the remaining bomber and caught up to it. A chopper outrunning a fixed wing aircraft. I'd call that slow, damned slow. Once the chopper caught up one of its crew fired a few clips into it from an M-16 he wasn't supposed to have according to the Field Marshall's voluminous rules of engagement and it too went down. The story of the Colts was told and re-told within "The Intelligence Community" for years in endless variations, many of them even more fanciful than the real thing. I heard it soon after I arrived at Ramasun. Didn't believe a word of it. Later translated a report from the Hmong on top of Bouam Long mountain, which has an excellent view of North Vietnamese territory; AN-2's were busy practicing bombing by dropping sandbags. Perhaps getting ready for another attack in 1970, but as far as I know they never made one. That same year we had a report of another possible enemy aircraft in the skies over Laos. I'm not going to tell you about that one as it has nothing to do with Bill Lair. If you want find out about it you'll have to read Chapter 10 of "Tales of Ramasun II" which is titled "Captain Midnight's Special Project".

When the report of the enemy bombing of Pha Thi hit Bill Lair's desk in Udorn he was dealing with the details of the collapse of Nam Bac. He already knew by that time that another disaster was on its way at Pha Thi. If the normally stodgy and predictable Viets were willing to try something as wild and crazy as pressing AN-2's into service as bombers what wouldn't they try. In another two months he'd find out what.

Recriminations and blame placing for Nam Bac were the order of the day in the Vientiane offices of the Field Marshall and the Ghost. They weren't the least bit worried about Pha Thi. They already had a foolproof master plan to defend it in the can. A huge weighty plan, reams and reams of it. A plan that was totally reliant on bombing. A plan that didn't even consider destruction of the TSQ-81 and evacuation of its staff…or anybody else. A mountain of bafflegab that would make any brave man who had to implement it weep…or turn to drink. The "key role" in the defense of Pha Thi was to be played by someone called the LADC which translated into English as "The Local Area Defense Commander" which sounded like it should be the local Hmong commander. A non-American guerilla chieftain in charge of defending a top-secret high-tech AMERICAN military installation? Well maybe not. Maybe the LADC was the American CIA field agent on top of the mountain who was supposed to be "commanding" the Hmong, though Bill Lair's agents were told never to command them. Or maybe it was the highest ranking "civilian" at the TACAN site. Or maybe it was the Air Force attaché in VT, though VT doesn't exactly sound "local". Or the commanding Colonel of Commando Club in Udorn. Now this LADC, whoever he was, was supposed to "coordinate" with the Embassy to call in airstrikes and the Ambassador would then "notify", or perhaps tell someone else to "notify", the 7th AF in Saigon and they would set up the strike and notify the TSQ-81 site commander who would notify the 7th AF...or something like that. And after all this coordination and notification was completed: "The 7th AF was to provide the strike forces as circumstances and time allowed. "As circumstances and time allowed" meaning "If we don't have anything better to do with our aircraft in South Vietnam." So why Saigon? Because South Laos was Saigon's "area of command" and Udorn's AOC was North Laos, got that? The Field Marshall's grand plan was outrageous, unworkable and downright laughable...in addition to being self-serving. There was no way anyone in Udorn or VT or Saigon or on top of Pha Thi would be able to follow it. It would take a team of Washington lawyers to decipher it.

Dick Secord had his own, much simpler, plan. Dick, the bomber guy, was more in accord with non-bombers Bill Lair and Pat Landry than he was with his own bureaucratically baffling superiors. His plan was cheap, quick, and easy to implement. A small contingent of US Army Special Forces, a few sergeants, an officer or two, all of them Vietnam battle hardened veterans, on top Pha Thi, and nowhere else. That would be enough when the worst came, and even Dick was now sure it was coming soon. Enough to do what needed to be done. To get the technicians evacuated, to get the TSQ-81 and all its supporting documents destroyed, and to get themselves out of there unharmed. The NVA could do what they wanted down in the valley. It would take them an hour or more to climb to the top of Pha Thi even if there was no defending fire or bombing. The Hmong could take care of themselves and disappear. They wouldn't need that long to get their job done. Dick got everyone on board except the (pardon my French) "FUCKIN' Field Marshall", who threw Dick out of his office when he broached the subject.

Not one to give up easily, Dick reviewed the backgrounds of the Americans already on the mountaintop. He thought that he could equip them and draw up an escape plan. What he found wasn't encouraging; none of them had any combat experience. He sent a message to Sullivan through the Ghost making a second proposal. Which the Field Marshall once again vetoed. Took it to his office himself and was thrown out a second time. Still not ready to give up he went to the commander of the 7/13th for weapons and training; got M-16's and ammo and set up weapons practice atop Pha Thi. He had gotten the 80 Thai PARU troops up top to strengthen defenses along with 105mm howitzers and 4.2-inch mortars. But even the best defense he could muster wouldn't solve all the problems of Pha Thi. The responsibility for its defense remained tangled. The rocky terrain of the mountaintop still impeded any organized defensive system and limited the number of defenders that could be deployed. The Field Marshall still insisted on interfering with anything that would improve the defenses of Pha Thi and considered any mention of evacuation defeatist. Dick Secord had done the best he could do considering the circumstances, but it wouldn't be enough.

Chapter 29: The Surprise Ending

When the final assault on Pha Thi came it wouldn't be what anyone, not even the NVA, expected. As of early February, it looked as if everything was proceeding according to NVA SOP (Standard Operating Procedure). Over in Vietnam the Tet Offensive had begun on 30 January 1968 which virtually insured that little air support could be spared for Pha Thi. So little support that no airstrikes were made on the main road leading into PT between February 2nd and 14th as NVA troops were swarming in over it. Vang Pao's spy net reported propaganda meetings during which the PL and NVA bragged about the coming assault and told them to get out of the way. An NVA Artillery Regiment, something never seen before in Laos, was brought up. One of VP's patrols ambushed an NVA artillery survey party killing them and sending their papers off to Bill and his crew in Udorn. The captured notebook had a bullet hole in the English word TACAN. The Taj Mahal was abuzz with activity. Bill presided over daily meetings of photo interpreters, signal intel spooks, and his own people as they worked together to record their findings in grease pencil on plastic covered map overlays. There was going to be the mother of all artillery bombardments by the NVA. Something on a scale never seen before in Laos.

By late February things looked better for the USA and worse for the DRV in South Vietnam, and a little better for the defenders of Pha Thi. The USAF was hitting the NVA hard now, doing a lot of damage, but Bill still wasn't convinced that PT could be held. Now even the Ghost had become a believer in the death of PT. A memo composed by Bill and his crew at Udorn went out from VT Station on 25 February under Ted Shackley's name saying that due to the success of the current bombing campaign PT would continue to be useable for another two weeks but:

"It is not able to predict, however, the state of security at Phou Pha Thi beyond 10 March because of the enemy's willingness to escalate his commitment in this area."

Sounds a little dry and mild to a civilian but I assure you something like this was hot shit by "Intelligence Community" standards. Dick Secord, as usual, put it less diplomatically:

"We had more evidence than any person ought to need to get the hell out of there or get reinforcements."

10 March was the pullout date for TACAN! But was anybody out there listening? Apparently not. Dick Secord's own outfit the 7th AF wasn't listening. They continued to repeat their party line. "Hold at all cost!" and its accompanying rationale- Commando Club was too important, was having too much of an effect on the enemy to be abandoned, was saving American lives. But what about the American lives on the summit of PT? Much bold talk from the desk bound brass, but no action. Business as usual while a huge powerful enemy force surrounded PT and prepared for the last act in its downfall.

On 9 March there were 19 Americans on top of Pha Thi. 16 sheep-dipped AF techies, 2 CIA men, and one FAC (Forward Air Controller). They met to work out a final evacuation plan which they were not allowed to implement without the approval of the Field Marshall in VT. They decided to make their way down a steep narrow path to a sandbagged bunker at the edge of a cliff near the helipad where they hoped to be picked up. A narrow ledge jutted out ten feet below the top of the cliff and they dropped a cargo net down to it so that it could be used as an emergency hiding place as it would be protected from enemy artillery shelling. Meanwhile in Udorn the 4802nd had gone into its own red alert mode. Bill had an important meeting with Thai officials to go to in Bangkok but put it off thinking the attack might come that night. Nobody went home. They had been bunking in the Taj Mahal for several days. When the worst didn't happen on the 9th Bill went off to his meeting the next morning.

On the evening of the 10th the senior CIA agent on Pha Thi reported that friendly troops were taking heavy casualties from artillery and rocket fire. Then the line went dead. Later he called back via a line through Long Cheng that an enemy artillery barrage had taken out the generator cables, the

105mm howitzer, the American barracks and the sandbagged bunker next to the helipad. Heavy clouds covered the mountain and the abandoned TACAN provided no guidance, so no effective air support was possible. At the overstaffed Taj things were going crazy until Pat took command. Ripping a phone off the wall in anger he then met briefly with Dick Secord; then the two of them went 'round the offices booting everyone out of the building until there were just three people left-Pat, Dick and Tom Clines. They gathered in Pat (and the absent Bill's) office and started working the radio telephones. It was something they'd done many times before but never for higher stakes than this. Trying to direct a battle many miles away by any means possible. Secord worked the USAF side. Trying to get a deadly C-130 "Snoopy" gunship that could rain down death in the form of thousands of rounds of 20mm cannon from the 7th at Tan Son Nhut. They put him on hold. Meanwhile Landry and Clines got VP at Long Cheng to order his single understrength reserve battalion to reinforce PT. When the NVA artillery barrage lifted after 90 minutes the American techies crawled up the cargo net from their protective ledge and went back to operating the radar which was undamaged, but it was no use, PT was socked in. By late evening things had quieted down. A few bursts of small arms fire were heard here and there. The defenses on the mountaintop were still in place and not heavily damaged except for the ones near the helipad.

The Zoomie Brass still refused to let PT evacuate. At midnight the Deputy Commander of the 7/13th contacted the Air Attache in VT saying that evacuation would only be considered as a last resort. Last resort? How much more "last" did he need? Dick kept pleading with Saigon for a gunship until they hung up on him. The Field Marshall in VT approved "a partial evacuation of Americans" whatever that meant, for 0830 hours on 11 March. VP had gathered reinforcements at Long Cheng. Choppers were standing by. All they needed to take off for PT was word from the Field Marshall, but no word came. At around 2 am NVA artillery roared to life again. At about the same time the senior USAF techie atop PT mountain called his boss, the commander of Commando Club in Udorn asking him for permission to blow up the site and get out. CC Commander Blanton told him that, if the hardware was still operational, he should get back to work.

At around 3 am the CIA agent at the helipad radioed Udorn to say he'd lost contact with the technicians at the TACAN site, was pinned down by enemy fire, and was hearing automatic weapons fire around the site. Landry and Clines had no doubt about it. There were NVA troops on **top** of Pha Thi. How in the hell did they get there? Meanwhile Dick was on the radio threatening to court martial a duty officer in Saigon if he didn't get a gunship to Lima-85. Somewhere along the line the helipad and much of the mountaintop came under both artillery and small arms fire so nobody could go anywhere.

While the Americans, Hmong and Thais on top of PT were enveloped in chaos 30 or so men from the North Vietnamese Army's 41st Sapper Battalion were methodically hunting down and killing the staff of the TACAN site. They had climbed the unscalable west side of Pha Thi in the middle of the night barefoot and in shorts and t-shirts using only wooden stakes, rope and grappling hooks. Disarming deadly booby traps as they ascended. They detached some of their men to pin down the Hmong and Thai troops while the rest made their way to the TACAN site on its lonely promontory and took it out before any of the friendlies on the mountain knew what had happened, then circled around to the west side of mountain to cut off the escape route of any survivors. At 5:15 am, after the damage had already been done on the summit of Pha Thi, Ambassador William Sullivan, the self-appointed Commander-in-Chief of all friendly forces in Laos, ordered its evacuation. Once the weather cleared the 7th AF out of Saigon, which had been so reluctant to provide air support, bombed the shit out of the summit of Pha Thi in case some of its top-secret codebooks or equipment were still intact.

There were seven American survivors, five techies and two CIA agents-one of them badly wounded. 14 American techies died, one American A-1 Skyraider pilot died when his plane was shot down while trying to attack the enemy. Choppers rescued all the Americans; Air America choppers not military choppers. No attempts were made to rescue any of the Thais or Hmong troops or villagers. It is not known how many of them died. The Hmong still held the base of the mountain when the battle was over. Since no one came to airlift them out they left on foot. Lieutenant Truong Muc of the 41st

Sappers and his men stayed on top of the mountain for a while but eventually came down. The families of the Americans killed were never notified where or how they died, much less who was responsible for the stupendously botched operation that got them killed.

The USAF, which wouldn't give Dick Secord a single C-130 gunship when it mattered, now piled on after the battle was lost. The NVA 148th Regiment, which had been the vanguard at Pha Thi, was pummeled by both the 7th and 13th AF's. One of its battalions was completely wiped out. The rest scattered. The bulk of the NVA 316th Division had seen little action and sustained only moderate casualties at Pha Thi. It headed south toward Nakhang, the place Bill Lair had recommended as a fallback site for the TACAN. The USAF bombed everywhere furiously and blindly, taking out its frustration on the enemy. And when LBJ suspended bombing north of the 20th parallel in Vietnam as a "peace feeler" it bombed even more. Bill reported "the skies were black with our aircraft". Requests for targets were pouring into the Taj Mahal. Bill and Pat didn't have enough targeting info to go around but that didn't matter. CIA men who were used to getting two or three airstrikes a day were dumbfounded. Dick Secord was overwhelmed; the USAF was giving him 300 sorties a day! They hadn't given him that many in a month before. So many bombs however badly targeted could not avoid killing some enemy as well as many civilians. They did kill lots of both and busted up lots of enemy roads and supply depots. Bill Lair was almost convinced that the Supermarket War would work, that the combination of Supermarket and his General Store would carry the day. It was easy for him to be a believer sitting in the Taj Mahal but when he went out into the field, he saw the truth. It wasn't working. VP and his Hmong were now hopelessly dependent on the US. The morale of Bill's elite Thai PARU was sinking. His long-time friend and PARU co-commander Pranet had thrown in the towel and gone back to Thailand and his old Police job. The death and destruction was mind-boggling but random. As soon as the USAF's haphazard rain of death slackened the NVA would be back just as strong and twice as determined as ever. They had their own vengeful scores to settle.

Chapter 30: A Prophet Has no Honor in his own Country

John 4:44 succinctly sums up what happened to Bill Lair after the tragic, senseless and idiotic battles of Nam Bac and Pha Thi. He had got it right. He had predicted what would happen. Therefor he had to be punished by the people who got it wrong. You may say that's awful. That he was a hero who should have been honored. But if **he** was honored what would happen to the folks who screwed up? Especially as all of them greatly outranked him. To be fair he wasn't the only scapegoat. Vang Pao was blamed, the Hmong were blamed, The RLA and the RLAF were blamed, The CIA was blamed, The Thais were blamed; Dick Secord blamed the 7th AF in Saigon and they blamed him and the 13th AF in Udorn, the Army Attaché in Vientiane was blamed for Nam Bac, the Air Force Attaché in Vientiane was blamed for Pha Thi, the weather was blamed. The Ghost backhandedly blamed Bill, and was blamed by the Field Marshall, who blamed everybody but himself.

After Pha Thi Bill Lair plunged into a period of deep depression and silence. His friend Pop Buell, a man who was in many ways his twin when it came to their views on Laos and the Hmong, was also deeply depressed, but that didn't keep the voluble and volatile Ohio farmer from talking. While Bill brooded Pop raged. I also have a sense of how Bill's moods worked gleaned from the recordings he made late in his life for the Veterans Archive Project which are the only way you can hear Bill now that he's dead. Even can see him as some of them were preserved on Youtube video. Bill had a decidedly manic-depressive streak like many great leaders. Like Abe Lincoln. Even more like Ulysses S. Grant. He was an active man with high highs and low lows. A man who was happiest when fully engaged in great works. Depressed, and sometimes even given to solitary drinking, during periods of inactivity and boredom. Like an Alaskan Husky who's happiest in harness pulling a heavy load, listless and peevish when confined to the kennel.

You can get an idea of Bill's ups and downs from his tapes. As a WWII soldier he's full of sharp details about the "hurry up" parts of his service, says little or nothing about the "waits". His year of combat from the Normandy Landing to the banks of the Elbe is a single breathless monologue of battlefield details, observations on the war and the people in it, thoughts on everything both relevant and irrelevant. What he and his crew were up to. What others were up to. His longer recounting of his CIA service flows the same way. Periods of detailed reporting and enthusiasm are followed by blank stretches he says little or nothing about. One of those blank periods is the months following Pha Thi. After a prolonged "high" burst of activity spanning nine months of Nam Bac and Pha Thi and post-Pha Thi bombing came a "low" stretch where nothing of note was happening. The NVA curtailed its offensive after it reached Nakhang. It was too late in the dry season for them to continue, but they clearly intended to do so during the next "fighting season". Vang Pao and his Hmong Army got a much-needed breather but knew they were going to be on the receiving end in four or five months.

Pop Buell's letters home were preserved so we know what he was thinking. In April '68 he wrote from Bangkok that he had finally made it to a city where "everyone you see is not scared to death" and "not afraid that tonight they will be killed, homes burnt or taken over by the Communists". He describes Hmong Country as "literally Hell". Sam Neua Province as lost, 25,000 people taken over by the Communists, another 10,000 fled from them to swell the already overcrowded camp he was running at Sam Thong. Later Pop went along with Vang Pao on a recruiting trip to try to fill the depleted ranks of his army noting:

"Thirty per cent of the kids were fourteen years old or less and about a dozen were only about ten years old. Another thirty percent were fifteen or sixteen. The rest were thirty-five and older. Where were the ones in between? I'll tell you, they are all dead."

Women outnumbered men by two to one in Hmong Country and worse was yet to come, much worse. Pop knew it, Bill knew it, but what could either of them do about it? Both were clearly thinking of what Vang Pao had said to Bill during their first meeting in early '61.

"We cannot live with the Communists. We must either fight them or leave. If you give us arms, we'll fight".

The "or leave" was never discussed in detail beyond VP's saying that his destination would be Sayaboury Province, and if the Communists pursued him there then on to Thailand. Sayaboury Province was on both Pop's and Bill's minds now. That odd, remote, sparsely populated, 6500 square miles of Laos on the wrong (west) side of the Mekong. Its northern half limestone karst mountains as rugged and heavily jungled as the remotest parts of Hmong Country. Mountains riddled with deep caves, rivers that disappeared underground, Tolkien's Middle Earth come to life in Southeast Asia. The southern half heavily forested hill country like the Ozarks but peppered with random chunks of higher mountains like the Appalachians. There were already Hmong living in Sayaboury Province. There were also Hmong living in the just as rugged country on the Thai side of the vaguely marked border. A border country so wild that 300 miles of it had but one road crossing. Only one legal way to leave or enter Laos in 300 miles!

Bill, and Pop might be able to do some good in Laos yet if they could help the Hmong flee to Sayaboury, but there was a problem. Now Vang Pao didn't want to flee. What both Bill and Pop had feared had happened. The Hmong had become dependent upon the USA for their survival, and VP had become dependent upon Uncle Sam for his political survival. They had both argued with him about it, but he was adamant. Said that if Sam Thong became unsafe, he'd set up a new refugee camp in a tiny corner of his fiefdom that was just as unsafe as Sam Thong. Yes, fiefdom, VP had gone from being a leader of Hmong Clans to becoming a warlord. Despite its trappings of nationhood Laos wasn't really a nation. Its national flag tells the story graphically. The three Elephants, the three-tiered parasol, the three-stepped platform. The three loosely united (and sometimes disunited) Kingdoms of Laos. Champassak in the far south, sometimes independent, more often a vassal state of the Khmer Empire. Vientiane, the largest and most powerful of the three still often menaced by neighboring Siam which grabbed two-thirds of it during the 1830's and renamed it Thai Isan. Luang Prabang in the northern mountains, smallest and weakest of the kingdoms, but most often independent due to its remoteness. The Royals of Champassak were still around more or less ruling their little kingdom in 1968. A Kingdom also called the 4th Military Region (MR4) of Laos. The Royals of Luang Prabang were still around too. Titular heads on the Kingdom of Laos but also the warlords of MR1. The Vientiane royals were mostly gone but some of their descendants were among the Generals and Colonels of MR5. There should have been five of everything on the Lao flag as the "modern" Laos had two additional "kingdoms". MR3, Central Laos, which was ruled of and on by General Phoumi, and MR2, Hmong Country, ruled by General Vang Pao.

VP was not about to abandon his "Kingdom" for ratty little Sayaboury Province (which was actually part of MR1), and he thought that he, and his people's, only hope was to stick with America. Bill and Pop knew better. Knew that the same America that would keep his people alive and fighting in the short run would lead them to destruction in the long run. Knew it and could think of nothing they could do about. Bill knew that he had lost his war in Laos. The man who had been called before the National Security Council just four years ago to explain his guerilla warfare plans had become a non-person. Ted Shackley's "Supermarket War" was triumphant. His "General Store War" was already dead, though not yet buried. There was nothing he could do about that either. The signs were clear. He had been consulted by the "Supermarket" players on both Nam Bac and Pha Thi, but they had ignored everything he told them. And when what he had predicted happened, they blamed him for their own negligence and wrongheadedness. Whispered that he'd "gone native", the ultimate Victorian racist putdown for a white man turned "colored". Said he knew too much about Thailand and Laos. Had become an enemy of American policy. If he stuck around in Laos, he'd be another Lord Jim, and the well-read Bill Lair knew it. By June of '68 Bill was done brooding. He had weighed all the plusses and minuses. He asked for a transfer. Out of Laos. Out of Thailand. Out of Southeast Asia. Bill Colby, who was then Saigon Station Chief, offered him a job as head of the shadowy Phoenix Program in South Vietnam. He turned it down. The Supermarket War folks were doing the same thing there as they were in Laos. It wasn't going to work there either. He knew it. He was so distraught, and heart-broken, that he hoped never to come back to the lands of which he was more expert than any other American. But he knew that his expertise was no longer wanted. The Secret War in Laos had been set on its course and policymakers in Washington no longer desired to be "confused by the facts" about Laos and Thailand. While Bill waited for his new assignment he hoped for the best. His idea of the best that might be available to him at this point was modest. He wanted to see "Station Chief" in his next title. He didn't care what city name came before it so long as it wasn't an Asian city. A small, quiet country would be nice. Perhaps Costa Rica. He was sure he could get his Spanish back up to snuff.

Part VI: Exile, then a "Special" Return - 1968-76

Chapter 31: A New Assignment

It was August of 1968 when Bill Lair and his family left Bangkok. He was leaving a lot behind. 18 of his 44 years of life in Thailand and Laos. All the many friends and acquaintances he'd made during those years. The many good things he'd done and the very few that hadn't worked out. Sent off to the Army War College at Carlisle Barracks, PA. He was a bit long in the tooth for "Mid-Career Training"; their course in Strategic Leadership was designed for Army men ranking between Major and Lt. Colonel mostly in their mid-to late-30s, but they admitted some civilians as well. Bill was the civilian equivalent of a Brigadier General. The course was described as:

"Graduate level instruction for mid-level military officers and civilians to prepare them for senior leadership assignments"

Bill hoped it would help him change careers within the CIA. To "do something completely different in another part of the world" as he put it. And he "would have gone if they'd sent me. But they didn't". With his course nearly completed he heard that Red Jantzen had finally moved on from Bangkok Station Chief after ten years and hoped he might be called. But he wasn't. He didn't know why, perhaps the badmouthing he'd gotten from the Field Marshall and the Ghost had something to do with it. After one year at the War College he was made Deputy Branch Chief for Southeast Asia, a high-sounding title but an empty job initialing reports and attending meetings. A comfortable office in the fancy CIA HQ at Langley. He ran into an old acquaintance from his early Thailand days in the cafeteria. One of the "old hands" when he first arrived in Bangkok. Now a couple of years from "30 and out" retirement with an empty title and an office like Bill's. Put out to pasture and hating every minute of it. Counting every minute of it. Ripping a page off his desk calendar each day to mark his long dull slog to retirement. They talked about the "good old days" in Thailand. Bill was sunk in gloom. Nearly ten more years to his 30. He'd never make it. He'd go stir crazy first. But what could he do? His unused college degree in Geology was surely worthless.

He sat at his lonely desk and read the latest traffic from Southeast Asia. The news wasn't good. The Tet offensive had shaken America both at home and on the battlefield. Anti-war demonstrators were everywhere in Washington, in huge numbers. The US began putting more pressure on Lao and Hmong forces "to do things they shouldn't have done to take the pressure off Vietnam" as Bill put it. To make the Hmong into conventional warriors. Guerilla warfare was no longer enough.

"That's the main reason I left Laos" Bill reflected "Shackley was making a big mistake pushing conventional stuff, but that's what Washington wanted him to do. I was the guerilla warfare guy. They didn't need me anymore. Pat could do the job as well as I could. I didn't want to be present at the funeral because I felt pretty sure it was coming."

Conventionalizing the war in Laos worked initially. Vang Pao's army retook the PDJ in early 1969 but couldn't hold it. Hmong casualties started to soar. The situation in Vietnam looked no better to Bill than the one in Laos. With Hmong forces decimated and RLA troops deserting in droves America brought in mercenary Thai troops by the thousands to fill the depleted ranks.

"I never believed we'd win in Vietnam" he moaned at one point though at other times he was mildly hopeful. Sometimes it seemed he wanted to win, even blamed the anti-war protesters for spoiling things, said that if the military had been left to do what it wanted to do without Washington interference, we could win…but he didn't believe his own arguments. Called Nixon's "Vietnamization" program "the right thing to do, but too late". Knew it was going to be a double funeral when the time finally came. Wanted that time to come soon but the war "dragged on and on with no end in sight". Even a visit from Vang Pao during the summer of '69 failed to relieve his depression. A CIA airplane took them off for a tour of Egelin AFB in Florida and cheered him up for a while. Then it was back to the gloom of reading dispatches at Langley and watching the latest anti-war demonstrations on TV.

****

Author's note: This is where I came in, with the conventionalization of the Secret War in Laos. A few months after Bill left Udorn I arrived at Ramasun Station ten miles down the road. Once I got there, the first intercepts I translated were about the retaking of the PDJ. I had my doubts about the Vietnam War but was still open to the possibility we might win it. Within six months I was as sure we were going to lose as Bill. After the cheering messages of early '69 things turned quickly sour. I cranked out translations on mutinies and desertions of RLA troops, sometimes whole companies. On mounting casualty counts. On mustered RLA and Neutralist battalions that had only a fraction of the men listed on their rosters. On bombings that killed more civilians than enemy. On new RLA battalions that appeared overnight. There was no BV45 (Volunteer Battalion 45) one night. A BV45 appeared as if by magic the next night. It took us several weeks before we found out that BV45 was a Thai battalion that had crossed the river and changed uniforms. We in the Laotian Translation Section at Ramasun were at the bottom of the intel food chain. Nobody above us told us anything unless they had something they couldn't figure out and needed our help. We didn't have "the need to know". By early '70 the Communists held at least 80% of Laos. By early '71 the front line in MR4 (South Laos) was at KM (kilometer post) 8 on the highway that led from the major southern town to Pakse to the Bolovens Plateau. On the very outskirts of the city. Five miles from the Mekong. Farther downriver I reported the NVA attacking the company sized RLA outpost of Moulapamok on the west side of the Mekong in Vaphikhamtong Province, a tiny piece of Laos on the "Thai side" of the river. A few weeks later I reported on an NVA battalion that crossed to the Thai side of the river. By the time I left the Army in June of 1971 I thought the whole thing would be over in six months, including Vietnam. A lot of other people at Ramasun thought the same. We were wrong about the timing but right about the result.

****

Red Jantzen's replacement as Bangkok Station Chief was Lewis H. Lapham (1921-99), a WWII Navy Veteran who used his GI Bill benefits to complete a

Master's in Public Administration before joining the CIA. He and Bill were CIA Basic classmates but then parted ways. Lou left the Agency after a year and used his Iowa political connections to get a Defense Department staff job in Washington. Later returned to the Agency in 1958 after getting a PHD in Pub-Admin from Harvard and was sent off to Paris for five years. By '64 he was in Saigon as Deputy Station Chief. Then on to Bangkok. He knew a lot about Vietnam but nothing about Thailand. Lou wanted Bill as his Deputy Station Chief for his Thai expertise, but the Agency brass vetoed it. No reason given. Not to be denied he asked them for Bill to fill his empty Chief of Ops slot. This time they caved. By late '70 Bill was back in Bangkok, but he wasn't quite done moving around yet. The Chief of Ops job was largely a paper-shuffling and personnel management gig that Bill was unsuited for. Both Lou and Bill knew that. Lou wanted Bill to provide him with the Thai expertise he lacked, not to sign requisitions. So, he created a job for him-Deputy Chief of Station for Special Activities. Lou showed how much he needed Bill by giving him the office next to his.

Bill found himself happy to be back in Bangkok living with family and friends, including some very influential Thai friends who made his new job much easier. There was his old pal, and co-commander of PARU, Pranet Ritruechai who had returned from Laos in 1967 disgruntled with the situation there, as was Bill, and had risen to the rank of General and Deputy Chief of the Royal Thai Border Police. A very good man to have as a friend as many of the "Special Activities" that would come Bill's way had some connection with the Kingdom's borders. Another good guy to know was Bill's first Thai friend from his Lopburi training camp days, Captain Sinay...now General Sinay and Chief of the Southern District of the Bangkok Metropolitan Police.

But Bill's best and most powerful friend was his brother-in-law "Sid". Siddhi Savetsila (1919-2015) was a mover and shaker in Thailand for more than 70 of his 96 years on earth. He was born into a rich, powerful, and accomplished family with a diverse and colorful background. His grandfather, Hugh Alabaster (1836-84), had been British Consul to Siam during the reign of King Mongkut (Rama IV) in the 1850s-60s and had married into the rich and powerful Bunnag family of Persian-Thai merchants and princes that dated back to the early 1600s when its founder, Sheikh Ahmad, arrived in the Ayutthaya Kingdom to set up shop. Sid's father was an advisor to King Chulalongkorn (Rama V) from the 1870s to the early 20th Century. After earning a degree in Metallurgical Engineering from MIT Sid became leader of the Free Thai Movement which fought during WWII against the Japanese and their Thai fascist stooges alongside the American OSS. After the War he joined the Royal Thai Air Force and rose to the rank of Air Chief Marshall, but his biggest impact was in the field of politics. He held many titles, everything from Foreign Minister to Member of the King's Privy Council, but much of his most important work was done behind the scenes. The Thais have an interesting word for that. Sid was a "Hanuman"(Hah-new-mon) after the half-monkey half-man shape shifting character in the Ramakien (the Thai version of the Hindu Ramayana-that almost endless collection of the more or less mythical tales of the contending forces on the Indian Subcontinent.) Hanuman is forever changing shape and showing up where and when he's least expected to save the day for the heroes and heroines of the tales. Brainy, sneaky, devious, and a bold fighter when he needs to be, Hanuman would make the idea CIA Agent. Or the ideal Thai politician. Both of Sid's sisters married American spooks. One married Willis Bird, an old OSS agent who stayed on in Thailand to found and run Bird Air, a private version of Air America that often worked under contract for Air-Am, or the CIA, or USAID or anyone else who needed cargoes of any kind delivered discretely to places no other airlines dared to go. The other sister, Chalern Bunnag Savetsila, married Bill Lair.

Chapter 32: Settling In

Having made his social rounds Bill got down to work. For the most part that work wasn't as demanding or exciting as his earlier work had been. He often found himself under-occupied and bored, but it wasn't anywhere near as dull as what he had been doing at Langley. There was the Communist insurgency in North and Northeast Thailand which had been sputtering along for two decades. The half-war he got into when he founded what became PARU in 1951. He was still a Thai Police Colonel and still co-commander of the PARU training base at Hua Hin. So Moon, who had been one of Bill's original PARU trainees at Lop Buri, came to him in 1971 wanting to become a pilot. By that time SEATO (Southeast Asia Treaty Organization) had established a flight school for Thai civilian pilots at Hua Hin. Bill got So into the school, even paid his tuition, and he did well. Later Bill came up with the idea of training Hmong pilots at the same place, then heard that the USAF was already training South Vietnamese to fly T-28's at Udorn so, with Vang Pao's support, he tried to enroll some Hmong there, but they wouldn't take them. "Primitives" couldn't be taught to fly, so the Zoomies contended. Undaunted Bill leased an abandoned Japanese airstrip across the Mekong from Vientiane, found two Piper Cubs gathering dust in Okinawa, and started a Hmong Flight school. He called his new operation Project 404. Hired So Moon as pilot trainer and got two Hmong up and flying. Finally turned out "30 or so" Hmong pilots, who became Aces. One of the Hmong Aces, Le Lu flew over 5000 missions. The Hmong flyers became heroes of their people.

Lou Lapham let Bill do "anything that came along and anything that no one else knew how to do". If he didn't know how to do it, he'd figure it out, or find some Thai who knew how to do it. 1972 brought the Munich Olympics and the Black September Terrorist Attack which you'd think would have nothing to do with Thailand. But it did. A secretary at the US Embassy in Bangkok was Lebanese and spoke Arabic. The CIA had the Lebanese Embassy bugged along with all the other Arab Embassies in Bangkok. Black September terrorists called the Lebanese Embassy in Bangkok to tell them that they had taken over the Israeli Embassy in Bangkok and were going to kill everybody in it unless a group of Palestinian prisoners was released. Lou came to Bill immediately. "What can we do about this?" Answer "Let me handle it." Bill rang up his old friend Sinay, the Bangkok Police Commander, and gave him the info. "Don't tell anyone where we got this info, Sinay." Answer "I won't tell a soul about it Bill. Will keep you informed." Sinay called the terrorists at the Israeli Embassy and sweet-talked them for several days. Offered them a flight out to the Middle East if they left their hostages unharmed. They wanted hostages to take with them to Egypt. Sinay gave them a Thai Air Marshall and a Deputy Prime Minister. Not many others could have done that. Nobody but Sinay according to Bill. Everything went as planned, and nobody knew a thing about it except Bill and Sinay. None of the Palestinian prisoners in Israel were released.

"The Thais are very good at that sort of stuff" mused Bill

You can say that again. Nobody in the world is better at "that sort of stuff" than the Thais. They've been doing it for centuries. Their military might may be shaky, and their war heroes are few. The real Thai heroes are their diplomats and negotiators, but you never hear about them because they are so good. When peace and order is threatened the USA sends in the Marines. Thailand sends in its elite corps of deal makers. And all Bill had to do to start the ball rolling was to make one phone call...to someone he knew was the right person.

Another of Bill's 'right people' was his old pal Pranet Ritruechai now Deputy Commander of the Royal Thai Border Police. He made many calls to Pranet over the years, most of them regarding the situation in Cambodia. The CIA knew absolutely nothing about what was going on there. Neither did anybody else except the Thai Border Patrol and they weren't about to tell anyone, except Bill. The RTBP knew so much because they were sending their own spies into Cambodia at tremendous risk. Want to spy on somebody really dangerous? You couldn't beat the murderous Khmer Rouge in that department. Anyone remember their leader Pol Pot declaring that "One Million is enough to build the New Cambodia"? Now there's a way to create a Socialist Utopia, start out by murdering five/sixths of your country's population. And they would have done it too. Bill kept the Agency up to date on the Khmer Rouge for years, made several trips to Phnom Penh to meet with the CIA's Station folks and the locals there. The situation was an even greater mess than either Laos or Vietnam. General Lon Nol's anti-communist government quickly lost control of the countryside. Was left trapped in Phnom Penh, Battambang and some of the provincial capitals, totally on the defensive and barely clinging to life. Phnom Penh Station poured beaucoup dollars into trying to field an anti-communist resistance movement but failed. A half-dozen guerilla armies, the Khmer Rouge being by far the largest and most powerful, were fighting each other. The US provided some support to the Thai Border Patrol and tried to get them to raise some resistance in western Cambodia near the Thai border, but they didn't want to do that. By the early 70's the Thais too had concluded that America was going to lose the Vietnam war and they didn't want to unnecessarily anger the Vietnamese Communists who they expected would soon become their new neighbors. Bill didn't think Cambodia had any promise as a place to make a stand. The people were willing, but not able, the Khmer Rouge had them too scared, too weak from starvation, and too tightly under control.

The USA was so sick of Southeast Asia by this time that it sat back and didn't lift a finger while Pol and his Khmer Rouge slaughtered over a million Cambodians. He probably would have reached his five million murders quota if our old enemies the Boys from Hanoi hadn't taken offense when he tried to invade newly re-united Vietnam over an ancient border dispute. The Viets ended up fighting a long drawn out anti-guerrilla war against the Khmer Rouge using captured American equipment, especially F-4 fighter-bombers, and conventional war tactics. The tables were now turned. Cambodia became Vietnam's Vietnam, a long grim grinding deadly battle. Laos wasn't the only place in Southeast Asia afflicted with the *Alice in Wonderland* malaise.

When there was nothing more pressing to do on his schedule Bill could always fight the War on Drugs. That never-ending unwinnable battle that's made many a career and ruined a few too. Once again Pranet was his go-to guy. A different border, Burma (I know, it's the unpronounceable Myanmar now, but it was Burma then. And still is, "Pha-mah" to most Thais.) The Burmese (Myanmar-eese?) side of the border was chock-a-block with opium growers and drug traffickers and heroin refiners. Business was brisk, as it almost always is in the opium trade. Thailand had made some progress in crop substitution, but Burma hadn't even tried. Probably couldn't have done much if they had tried as the Rangoon government didn't control the Drug Lords' area.

The Drug Lord of the hour was a Chinese named Lo Sing Han who had been given the nickname "Khun Sa" (Master Dope). He was active in an area close to the Thai border. Sometimes went back and forth over a trail that crossed briefly into Thai territory. The Thai Border Police had spies in the villages near his trail. Bill hung out with them for a while. Also kept the DEA and his former Agent "Nature Boy" Bill Young informed. Between the lot of them they snatched Khun Sa during his five-minute passage through Thai territory and turned him over to the tender mercies of Thai Police HQ in Bangkok. Once again, the Thai negotiators came to the fore and made a deal with the Burmese Generals to pass him off to them. They said they'd bring him to trial, but they didn't. In the meantime, one of his former associates took his place so he might as well have been in jail. Another drug battle won, make way for the next.

Chapter 33: The War Drags On

While Bill was engaged in his "Special Activities" he had plenty of time to read the latest Agency reports and Ramasun intercepts. The news between 1971 and 1975 varied from bad to worse. The first of the bad news arrived before he left Langley for Thailand. In February of 1970 the NVA attacked Pop Buell's Sam Thong refugee camp obliterating it and sending some 30,000 Hmong non-combatants off to the west where they stayed in "the wilderness" for two months before returning to find everything they, and Pop, had built during the last half-dozen years, destroyed. His 100-bed hospital destroyed. His schools and his Sam Thong University destroyed. His experimental plots and the Hmong gardens ravaged. The returnees picked among the rubble to salvage vegetables that weren't smashed or full of shrapnel. Even after their return the NVA continued to fire 122mm Soviet WWII rockets down on the camp killing dozens. Long Cheng was also attacked but held.

By January of 1971 Bill was at his Bangkok Station job when the next NVA attack on the Hmong began to build. He got a call from Doctor Charles Weldon (1920-2002), the head of the hospital at Sam Thong, asking for help in defending Pop Buell's huge refugee camp. Vang Pao would no longer provide troops this time around. His situation at Long Cheng was too desperate. Dr. Weldon was a long-time acquaintance. They had both arrived in Laos in 1961. He wasn't aware that Bill no longer was chief of paramilitary operations in Laos or that he was now working for Bangkok Station. Bill sent him the intrepid Jack Shirley to organize whatever troops he could pull together. Jack went back to Laos for the first time in four years and improved the camp's internal security and nighttime surveillance enough to withstand small unit enemy raids and sabotage but could do no more than that. After much argument among Pop, Doc Weldon, the Hmong Clan leaders, and VP it was decided to evacuate Sam Thong before the NVA arrived. USAID had an abandoned worksite with several large buildings, a 3,000-foot runway, and road connections to Vientiane at Ban Xon. Most of the Sam Thong Hmong were airlifted there before the NVA attacked Long Cheng, though some returned to their home villages even if they were now under Communist rule, and some lit out for Sayaboury Province.

At this point nobody cared who did what in Laos. The Blonde Ghost and the Field Marshall were both long gone along with the troublesome backstabbing Red Jantzen. Anyone from any US agency who wanted to advance his career had cleared out. Just the old-timers like Bill, and Pop, and Doc Weldon, and Jack Shirley to run what was left of the collapsing show. The old-timers were the only ones left who gave a shit about the Hmong or the Lao or all the other natives…or Laos.

Beginning on March 17, 1971 the NVA pounded Vang Pao's Long Cheng HQ with their newly acquired Soviet 130mm howitzers. They were more powerful and had a longer range than the biggest American gun the Hmong had; the venerable WWII 155mm howitzer. Their gunners were, as always, highly accurate. They pulverized everything above ground and drove the defenders of Long Cheng into a warren of underground caves and bunkers. Americans at Long Cheng were now being shuttled back and forth to Udorn every night to keep them from getting killed or captured. The NVA never launched any serious attacks during the day. With no American air controllers to guide them F-4 Phantoms attacked what they thought was an NVA assault descending from Skyline Ridge behind the camp, but it was actually a Hmong assault going up the ridge to attack the NVA. The result came to be called "St. Valentine's Day Massacre". Most of the troops killed by the Phantoms were Hmong. Vang Pao was so angry he threatened to quit the US and go off on his own. An idle threat as what was left of his army, and his people, were now hopelessly dependent on the USA. Hmong morale, already low, sank still further. The morale of the Americans on the ground at LC wasn't much better.

After the "Second Battle of Long Cheng" Vang Pao's army was so feeble and demoralized, and so short of men, that the US dispatched RLA and Thai mercenary troops to keep Hmong HQ from being crushed the next time the NVA came calling. RLA troops to fill the Hmong ranks? The ultimate insult to

Hmong fighting prowess. And sure enough "Long Cheng III" did arrive, even earlier than usual, on 04 January 1972. There were far fewer refugees to flee this time and they did so on their own. Scattering into the mountains in hope of survival somewhere, somehow. The NVA once again pounded Long Cheng's ragged defenders with artillery and once again captured Skyline Ridge. VP no longer had enough troops to attempt a counterattack. An attack by RLA battalions surprisingly re-captured the ridge, but soon they were chased back down, after which they mutinied and demanded to be airlifted back to Vientiane. A few weeks later Thai mercenary troops took the ridge and held it. The monsoons arrived and the NVA had to pull back leaving behind the bodies of some of their troops who had starved to death. When you're up against any enemy who'll fight until he starves to death you know you're in trouble. There would be still one more "Battle of Long Cheng" but that would not be for a while yet. When it came it was truly pathetic...and Vang Pao and the Hmong lost.

In all the recordings he made for the Vietnam War Archives and all the speeches he would later make Bill Lair never mentioned anything about these tragic events. Perhaps they were too painful for him to talk about. Perhaps the fact that he could do nothing to reverse the slow-motion death spiral of "his" Hmong people silenced him. In the end he did get a chance to help them but that would not come for some time yet.

By late 1972 it became clear to all but the dullest observers of events in Laos that the Communists were not in a hurry to take it over. They already controlled a good 90% of its land, though probably less than half of its people, many of whom were now internal refugees within what little was left of their own country. Hanoi was no longer looking west to Laos but south to Saigon. Once Saigon was taken, they'd get back to Laos. And to take Saigon they'd need all the troops they could muster, including as many troops as they could safely pull out of Laos. Their solution? A retread of the 1962 Geneva Accords. This time they'd even pull most of their troops out of Laos...temporarily. A nice peaceful cease-fire in place (since they controlled almost all of Laos) and a revival of the old Tripartite government would do them just fine. By February 1973 they got their cease-fire, same terms as in

'62 except no International Control Commission to pretend to enforce those terms.

With the cease fire in place the contending parties spent a peaceful year and a half of wrangling and finally produced an odd beast called the Provisional Government of National Union (PGNU). It looked pretty much like the old Tripartite Government except that the Neutralists and Royalists had much less power and the Communist PL had much more. The highwater point of this new era of peace and unity was reached in May of 1974 when the leader of the Communist PL, "The Red Prince" Souphanouvong, put forth an 18-point plan for National Reconstruction and Reconciliation that promised free elections, democratic rights, respect for religion, and 'constructive economic policies'. The ink was barely dry on his proclamation when things began to take a bad turn, and once they had turned, they kept on getting worse. Neutralist Prince Souvanna Phouma was still Prime Minister but he saw the 'handwriting on the wall' and, after he'd had a heart attack, he retired to France for medical treatment, never to return. The Red Prince, now Acting Prime Minister, demanded USAID submit their projects and funding to his oversight and control. They yielded to him in part, turning over three million dollars' worth of equipment that was being used for road and dam construction projects. Then they evacuated all foreign construction workers effectively shutting down those projects. He allowed USAID humanitarian aid programs to continue at current levels under his oversight, but not control. By September of '74 demonstrators began to appear in the streets of Vientiane and other cities. Some vaguely demanded 'reform' and an end to 'corruption' echoing the anti-Junta demonstrators that so often appeared on the streets of Bangkok. Others demanded 'peace, rice and land' echoing Lenin's Bolsheviks 'peace, bread and land'. Still others were RLA soldiers demanding to be paid. They hadn't been paid for more than a year since the US cut military funding to Laos. Few if any of them were still on duty, yet they were desperate enough to hope somebody would pay them. The most organized and most insistent demonstrators were clearly orchestrated by the Communists. They demanded that all Americans and other assorted Capitalist Exploiters leave the country immediately. Their speeches and pamphlets were lifted word for word from the propaganda broadcasts of "The Voice of the Free People of Laos" beamed in from Kunming, PRC. The style of the language sounded much more Chinese than Lao. Many wealthy people and business leaders began to move their assets, and themselves, out of Laos. Thousands of people who had nothing to move but themselves began to cross the Mekong as well.

Which brings us to April of 1975. Bill has already received a Ramasun intercept reporting that Hanoi wants to capture Saigon before Ho Chi Minh's birthday of May 19. They are poised to get there a bit early (on April 30). They are also now bombarding, though not attacking, Long Cheng with their 130's. No military or CIA Americans are left in Laos. No American bomber has flown over Laos since the cease-fire was signed in '73. Even USAID and Pop Buell's IVS are gone. No Americans are left in Laos except a skeleton crew of low-ranking diplomats at the US Embassy. The US Ambassador is long gone. Endgame in both South Vietnam and Laos is approaching. Bill Lair doesn't know it yet, but he is about to get a chance to do something for his Hmong.

Well maybe not quite "No Americans". There is one unofficial American still in Laos. An American CIA agent named Jerry Daniels (1941-82) who goes by the nickname "Hog". Hog is in Laos in defiance of his own Agency's orders. The official position of the CIA at is that it will have nothing to do with any Lao or Hmong refugees. That those refugees, especially the Hmong, are unfit to be taken into America because they would be unable to adapt to American life. That the men who were America's only effective anti-Communist fighting force in

Laos, and their families, are unwelcome in the USA. That they are somebody else's problem. Maybe the Thais, maybe USAID, maybe the UN High Commission of Refugees (UNFCR), but not the CIA. Later the Lords of Langley will change their tune, will even come close to taking credit for refugee evacuation, but those who were on the scene in Laos and Thailand know that is a lie. The most unsung American heroes of this final act of the Secret War are Bill Lair and "Hog" Daniels.

Young (17) Hog Daniels became a smoke jumper in Montana as soon as he graduated high school in 1958. Two years later he was in Laos as a "kicker" for Air America; rigging parachutes and kicking rice bags out the doors of everything from tiny Helio Couriers to lumbering C-46's over Hmong Country. Of all the dangerous jobs you could do in Laos kicker was the most dangerous. But Hog loved it. He was an adrenaline junky. He was also one very brainy dude. He stayed a kicker until 1965 and spent his free time absorbing Lao and Hmong languages and culture. In '65 the brawny brainy young man caught Bill Lair's eye and he made Hog a Junior Case Officer. "Junior" because he didn't meet the education requirements for the job, though he knew more about Laos and its people than many "senior" Agents with degrees from the finest colleges. If Bill hadn't been given a free hand (and purse) to run Momentum, he could never have gotten away with hiring Hog, who took the additional code name "Sky" after his native Montana upon being named a Junior Agent

During the next five years Junior Agent "Sky" was on the scene of most of the Secret War's hotspots. In 1970 Bill assigned Sky as personal case officer to General Vang Pao at Long Cheng. He and the General became fast friends and Hog came to know everyone who was anyone in the Hmong army as well as many of its grunts. While the NVA pounded Long Cheng and all the other Americans shuttled back and forth every night to Udorn for safety Hog usually remained behind hopping the shuttle flight only when he had something important to report to his boss Bill Lair. Between 12 and 14 May 1975 Hog managed the evacuation of Vang Pao, his large family, and most of his officers and their families, a total of approximately 2500 people, from a Long Cheng that was under bombardment and in its death throes. Air America flew them out. It is unclear whether this desperate operation was approved by either Langley HQ or Vientiane Station Chief Daniel Arnold. Most of those involved in it say it wasn't.

It was certainly a low point in the military careers of Vang Pao and his officers. VP was deserting his own troops at Long Cheng the same way RLA Prince General Bounchanh had deserted his own troops at Nam Bac. But Hog, and Air America, weren't done yet, over the next weeks they evacuated another 12,000 Hmong from Laos. Kept airlifting people out until there was no place left to put them in Thailand.

At this point Bill Lair got into the evacuation act. Bill was a straight arrow when it came to following Langley's orders even when he disagreed with them, which he often did. But when Hmong refugees began to touch Thai soil they were in his jurisdiction, or rather the jurisdiction of his boss Bangkok Station Chief Lou Lapham. And if this wasn't a "Special Activity" then there was no such thing as a Special Activity. Bill went to Lou for permission to work the "refugee problem". Lou gave it. Next stop brother-in-law Sid. The official position of the Thai Government wasn't much different than the official position of the CIA. "We don' wan' no steenking refugees". Bangkok's political generals, the ones who were more familiar with a 9 iron than an M-16, raged against any and all refugees. "Shoot 'em" "Turn 'em back" were their rallying cries. But the refugees were already arriving in droves by air, and by water across the full 1000-mile length of the Thai/Lao Mekong border.

Sid set to work on the Bangkok politicians-in-uniform with (perhaps) the covert aid of the biggest "player" of them all in Thailand HM King Bhumibol. Bill never says what exactly it was Sid did. He probably didn't know all, or even most, of what he did, but whatever it was it worked. Meanwhile Bill made his way up to the Khon Kaen HQ of the Royal Thai Border Police and huddled with its Deputy Commander his old PARU pal General Pranet. It was nice to have friends in high places, especially the right high places.

Vang Pao and his 2500 were quickly hustled out of Thailand. Bill met the General at the US Embassy in Bangkok and was appalled. The once great leader of his people was now shrunken, overweight and shaken. Passive and confused he was a ghost of his former self shuffling along to wherever he was pushed. Hog Daniels got VP and his people airlifted across the Pacific to his home state of Montana where he found them digs in rented housing near Missoula. The other 12,000 first-wave Hmong refugees were jammed into an abandoned US Marine Airbase at Nam Phong near Khon Kaen. Bill asked brother-in-law Sid if he could find them a roomier place with enough land so they could grow gardens and keep themselves fed and occupied.

"We have to get them off that base, Sid. They're packed in and nobody's doing anything for them. We've got to do something."

Sid found a tract of land in a mountain valley of Loei Province not far from the border of Laos. The Interior Ministry provided 400 acres of scrubby forest and the Army sent a Colonel and 80 men to clear it. The troops sarcastically christened it "Ban Vinai". "Vinai" meaning "orders". The camp we were ordered to build. The Ban Vinai Refugee Camp got its first 4,000 refugees, 90% of them Hmong, in October 1975. Another 8,000 from the overcrowded temporary camp at Nam Phong arrived with the next few months. When Hog Daniels returned from settling VP and his crew in Montana, he went work at Ban Vinai helping to organize the rapidly expanding camp. Had to keep expanding it to accommodate the Hmong refugees that kept arriving over the next months, and years. Eventually over 50,000 Hmong were sent to the US and smaller numbers were sent to other countries including Australia, Canada, France...and even French Guiana. They did have a hard time adapting in their new homes, except in French Guiana which was a virtual replica of Hmong Country. Had a hard time, but they were tough, and they survived, and once they had survived, they prospered, prospered modestly but prospered.

Hog Daniels stayed on in Thailand and was personally responsible for getting them across the Pond to the US. He carried the whole load at first. Later USAID picked up some of the slack. Still later the UNHCR's top-heavy bureaucracy began to operate. The CIA said they provided funding, but Bill wasn't happy with his Agency's effort. Also thought USAID's contribution was "not the best". As far as Bill was concerned the only American who came off well in the whole refugee effort was the Hog.

"He was an awfully good man. Worked with us in Laos for a long time. Stayed with the Hmong at the refugee camps for months at a time without coming out for any kind of rest. He knew all of them."

One thing the Hog did that no one else would tackle was to prepare the paperwork families needed to satisfy the myriad requirements for entry to the US. He was the only American in the camps who was fluent in both Hmong and Lao, so he did much of the interviewing. His paperwork was often highly creative. The Hmong brought no papers with them, had none to begin with. Hog made them all up to fit what the US wanted to see from refugees. The US wanted nice nuclear American-style on-paper families so that's what he gave them. Never mind that there was no such thing as a nuclear family in Hmong Country. Or that the Hmong were polygamous, and as the casualties of war left them with more than two women for every man, and women were not allowed to live without a man, almost all men had more than one wife. The Hmong "families" were clans, beyond even American extended families. Hog neatly packaged Hmong families for American consumption in groups of people who wanted to stick together. Husbands and wives might become brothers and sisters. Daughters might be "mia noi", second wives. Sons might be second cousins. Grandmothers might be Aunts and vice-versa. Some "families" were cobbled together from people who had no blood relationship. Since no one had any marriage papers Hog officially married them. Since no one had birth certificates he created them. Some of the Americans working in the camps knew what he was doing but were afraid to do such things themselves. Others were clueless. Nobody even knew what Hog's official position in the camps was. His title was "Ethnic Affairs Officer" but he was paid by the CIA. Bill saw to that.

Hog Daniels stayed on in the camps until he died tragically in 1982. Cause of death officially reported to be gas from a faulty water heater in his Bangkok apartment. Conspiracy theories abound regarding his death. That he didn't die, he disappeared, either voluntarily or forcibly. That he went underground. That he later was spotted in the US and Europe. That he was murdered by the CIA or the Communists or a disgruntled Hmong who tried to bribe him to get this family priority passage to the States and was refused, or by a mystery man who had been threatening to kill him for some time. There were other rumors that included homosexual liaisons, alcohol poisoning and suicide. Daniels had been on a drunken binge when last spotted alive. Something that often occurred when he made one of his infrequent 'R and R' trips to Bangkok. His body had lain in the broiling unairconditioned apartment for three days before it was discovered. It was sent back to the States in a sealed coffin which authorities refused to open. The Hmong community in Missoula honored their 'Mister Hog' with an elaborate 3-day funeral which was attended by hundreds of Hmong and Americans including Vang Pao, CIA agents, Old Smoke Jumpers many of whom "pushed cargo" in Laos, and old school chums.

Jerrold "Hog" Daniels was the first non-Hmong ever honored with such a funeral.

Chapter 34: Thailand Sunset

After the "refugee problem" of 1975 was on its way to being solved Bill Lair's CIA career, and his days in Thailand, were numbered, but a final "special activity" came his way in early '76. This time he didn't have to go looking for it. It came to him. His brother-in-law Sid had left the Royal Thai Air Force for a job at the Ministry of Foreign Affairs (he would later become Minister of Foreign Affairs from 1980 to 1990). Thailand was pursuing its age-old strategy of "navigating the river". Sometimes you go with a powerful ally; you steer close to one bank. Other times, when you have no strong allies and are surrounded by potential enemies you head for the middle of the river. Thailand had steered close to the US bank since WWII. Now, with the US defeated, discredited, and pulling out of Southeast Asia, it was edging toward midstream. As a part of that change of course the Kingdom was trying to warm up ties with Beijing.

Sid was part of a Thai "good will" delegation that travelled to Beijing in early 1976. While they were there, they were honored with a visit to an obviously ailing Chairman Mao. He didn't have much to say to them, but they picked up a good deal of information on the struggle and plotting that had already begun among factions and individuals to determine who would replace him. Sid was ready to pass that information to Bill, and to no one else. He knew that he could trust Bill to deliver it to where it was needed without revealing where he got it. The American Intelligence Community knew nothing of what was going on behind closed doors in Beijing. As far as they knew Mao was still in good health and fit to rule. His illness and incapacity were a closely kept PRC state secret. Mao lingered on for months before dying on September 9, 1976. By the time he died his successor had already been decided.

No more "special activity" scoops after that. Bill had decided to take the earliest possible CIA retirement in mid-1976 at age 53. Many CIA case officers went "30 and out", the field was no country for old men. Bill could have stayed on in the same kind of empty "go to meetings" HQ job he left to return to Thailand but chose not to. He preferred the field and knew that there was no longer any place there for him .

Before he left Thailand, James William Lair had one last event to attend. A royal audience with HM King Bhumibol Adulyadej. The two so very different men had been meeting each other informally for the last 24 years. Ever since Bill set up the PARU training center across the road from HM's Hua Hin Palace. So very different...but in some ways the same. Both quiet and close-mouthed. Both stiff and proper in public. Both able to keep a secret. Both working behind the scenes, often indirectly. His Majesty would have made a great CIA agent. Bill might have made a decent King, at least he knew how this King worked, and how many good things he did.

While Bill received the highest honor available in Thailand, he doesn't mention any honors or farewells from the CIA in which he served with distinction and brilliance for 27 years (he got 3 years credit toward retirement from his WWII Army service). No offers of continued employment. No sweet plums of consultancies or memberships in any of Washington's military or foreign policy think tanks. By the looks of it, the CIA was either glad to see him go, or didn't care one way or the other. Nothing like the honors Ted Shackley received when he left the Agency a few years later. Nothing like the honors and acclaim showered on "Field Marshall" Bill Sullivan when he retired from the Foreign Service.

By the time Bill had had his audience with the King of Thailand the Secret War in Laos was over and the Kingdom of Laos was dead. It officially expired on December 2, 1975, though it had been effectively dead for at least six months before that. Refugees of all tribes and ethnic groups flooded across the border to Thailand which was now officially closed by the Communist victors and would stay closed for the next 17 years. The victors murdered, worked or starved to death most of the Lao Royal Family including King Sri Savang Vathana, who had naively opted to stay behind in hopes that the new government of the Peoples Democratic Republic of Laos (PDRP) would honor the pledges of the Red Prince Souphannavong's 18 Point Plan; which it had no intention of doing.

"Social parasites" including Buddhist monks, prostitutes, anyone who worked for the Americans, any RLA or Neutralist soldier above the rank of private, any business person no matter how small, and many schoolteachers were packed off to the "Seh-meh-nah" (Seminars) to be re-educated. Most of the "students" in these thinly disguised concentration camps either died or fled before they could complete their "courses". A pogrom was launched against the Chinese population and they were driven out of Laos. Hanoi didn't want their Communist 'comrade' China to grab Laos. With good reason as it proved since the Chinese Red Army tried to invade Vietnam in 1979 (and was defeated). For two decades Laos was occupied by Vietnamese troops who created a puppet government headed by officials most of whom were at least half Vietnamese.

As the Viets were strapped for cash they got the Soviets to return and fund a few big projects, mainly ugly Soviet-style buildings, and a massive cotton growing project south of Vientiane that cleared dozens of villages to build a collective farm and cotton mill. I rode past it in 1994 on my first visit to Laos in 23 years. Some spindly volunteer stalks of cotton were almost lost among the weeds of thousands of acres of untilled chemically poisoned fields. The only activity at the vast sprawling cotton mill was a few guys with sledgehammers busting holes in its concrete walls, presumably to remove the equipment and sell it for scrap. Vientiane was a near-ghost town in '94. The people in the rest of the country seemed on the verge of starvation. Tens of thousands had starved to death in earlier years. I read an article in a Bangkok newspaper that claimed that as many as 800,000 people had eventually fled Laos after the Communist takeover. Roughly one fourth of its estimated pre-takeover population. Official figures are nowhere near that high, but official figures don't include the many Lao who crossed the border to Thailand and blended in with the population of Isan (the northeast). The author of the article estimated that number at "around 400,000". A number I find easy to believe as I've met many of them in Isan and heard about others.

While Laos starved the American human "debris of war" began to gather in Bangkok as early as 1975. Some of the CIA case officers who served in Laos and Thailand like Pat Landry had enough years in to retire. Others quit. Few went back to Langley. There was nothing for them there. CIA guys who spent their lives working on the front lines in the field were not considered promotable and there were no other wars for them to go to for a time. Most of them were already too old for more wars anyway. Pat fared better than most. He was legally married to a Thai woman so he could run a business in Thailand. "Foreigners" were barred from owning or running businesses in Thailand in 1976, and still are banned now. They get around this difficulty by marrying Thai citizens and attributing any business they do to them. Pat opened a bar in Bangkok that was frequented by washed-up CIA agents and assorted American expats. It did quite well. Later he got into several other businesses and moved to Chieng Mai. The rest of the old spooks and spies drifted from the whores of Patpong Road in Bangkok to the whores of Pattaya Beach. Drinking too much. Fucking too much. Spinning tales to each other. Crying in each other's beer. Bitter about the way things came out. Bitter about the way the Agency treated them. Some tired of city life and drifted up to the Isan, especially Udorn, where they found life quieter and cheaper. Few of them did anything particularly notable after they left the Agency.

But Bill Lair, who'd spent more time in Thailand and Laos than any of the others, was gone by June of 1976. While most of them remained in Thailand for the rest of their lives, or only returned to the US when they were in failing health and needed medical care. He and his family went back to his native Texas. He said his leaving was "not a difficult decision". That he "wanted to get the kids back to the US". Also said that he was sad to leave Thailand and "sad to see the way things were going" (in Southeast Asia). Just "sad" not bitter like his fellow old spooks who stayed on. He clearly was having trouble putting a brave face on his own service, and his prospects, remarking "But you know, I can get along" and concluding that "I figured I did the best I could".

Part VII: An Uneasy Retirement -1976-92

Chapter 35: Back to Texas

Bill returned to Texas and bought a ranch near Meridian in Bosque County. A chunk of the Old Texas that reminded him of his youth. Perhaps he wanted to relive the scattered good times he had during that chaotic and troubled youth. The times he'd spent with his grandfather W. H. Lair on his small hardscrabble ranch near Claude. Not many people, 1,400 or so in the town of Meridian, 17,000 in the County. Central part of the state, well away from any big cities. The beautiful rolling Texas Hill Country. Not that far from Waco, where his mother had worked for the VA. The old cold warrior came home to his roots. His oldest child, Lehta Chalern Lair (1956-) went off to college, a Texas public university like her father, in the Fall of '76. His son James William Lair II (1961-) would later attend his old alma mater of Texas A & M. His wife Chalern Savetsila Lair (1930-96) lived with him on the ranch until she died. In his 2001 interview with the Vietnam Archives Project which took place at his ranch five miles outside of Meridian he tells the touching story of his trip back to Thailand to have her remains properly buried. Goes into great details as to how it is done and how important it is. Details I know well as my wife is also Thai.

Earlier in this book I likened Bill to U.S. Grant. Both were quiet, deep-thinking creative men. Both manic-depressive men with great energy in times of crisis. Both men saw people of other races and backgrounds for the human beings they are, and not the stereotypes that their own white fellow Americans put upon them. Both were easily underestimated. Both won great victories and suffered great defeats; and bounced back from those defeats. And, unfortunately, both were lousy businessmen. Bill's Lair and Son ranching venture failed. Failed so badly that he couldn't pay off all his debts even after selling most of the land. He could have gone back to Thailand and used his many high-ranking contacts to make big money. Maybe even the kind of money his American brother-in-law Willis Bird was making with his Bird Air. Thailand's economy boomed after the end of the Vietnam War. Bill knew that all foreign-owned businesses of any size needed insider contacts to be successful there. Thailand was, and still is, a society governed by men, not laws. There's no law on the books in Thailand that cannot be circumvented with a bit of help from the "right people". If Bill didn't know the right people, he knew the people who knew them.

He could have sold himself out in Thailand for a pot of gold, but he didn't. It wasn't his style. He had too high a respect for the good straight Thai people he met to pander for wealth in their country. Unsure of what to do with himself he saw an advert for independent truckers to deliver recreational vehicles from a Texas factory to dealers around the country. Bought an International 4080 Cummins-powered Diesel and a 54-foot flatbed trailer and went into business. Perhaps a strange move for the most successful spook of the Vietnam War, but somehow it was the sort of thing a man like Bill Lair would do. The sort of thing a proud yet humble, independent, moral man would do. So off he went for three or four days a week, the equivalent of a retired Brigadier General driving a big rig across the highways and byways of America. Ridin' high in the cab. Did he ever tell any of his fellow truckers about his earlier incarnation in Southeast Asia while chowing down at some pit stop on the wide-open plains? If he did, did they believe him?

He had a lot of time to think about what could have been in Laos if he and the "few good men" of Momentum had run the war the way he, and they, had wanted to run it. Their Country Store could have triumphed over Shackley's Supermart. A few million dollars wisely spent could have staved off defeat where billions bought nothing but death, destruction and disaster. The Hmong could still be in their mountains living the way they wanted to live. Much of Laos would not be the ravaged poisoned landscape it still is. A landscape so full of mines and unexploded bombs that it is still maiming and killing a hundred or more innocent people a year fifty years after the last bomb was dropped.

He mulled over the mistakes he'd made. Blamed himself for not arguing Vang Pao out of defending Padong. Not putting his foot down. He held the purse strings. He could have done it. But it ran against his philosophy of not telling the Hmong, or their leader, what to do, even when he knew their decisions were wrong. That VP would learn from his mistakes. But he didn't learn from Padong and kept making the same kind of mistakes until he nearly destroyed his people. Blamed himself for not insisting that VP set up the escape route through Sayaboury Province that he'd vaguely hinted at during their first meeting in January of 1961. Maybe he should have gone ahead and set up such a route himself, then forced VP to take it when the time came to either get clear of the NVA or get out of Laos.

As the mileposts clicked past Bill rehashed the things he could have done differently. The things that might have worked out but didn't. But in the end, he could see that it wouldn't have made any difference. America was bound and determined to fight its own kind of war in Southeast Asia. The big bucks, big boom, high-tech, conventional, Korea-style war that had no chance of success in South Vietnam, or Cambodia, or Laos. We did things the American Way and made a bloody mess of it. His way had worked in the beginning, but by 1968 Bill's way had been cast aside.

And when the whole futile stinking mess was over in Laos in 1975 the US, and the Agency, had intended to turn their backs on the Hmong and leave them to suffer the horrible consequences of being our loyal ally in that now lost war. Henry Kissinger wasn't joking when he said, "To be an enemy of the US might be dangerous, but to be its friend **is** dangerous." And we would have abandoned the Hmong if Bill and Sid and Pranet and Hog, and a handful of Thais and Americans acting **against** the official stated interests of their own governments hadn't prevented them from doing so. One good thing had been done in Laos after 1968. Only one. And, after all Bill's soul-searching he could conclude that what he had said when he left Thailand in 1976 was still true. "I figured I did the best I could." Bill's 'best he could' helped save thousands of Hmong lives. Lives that his own government, and the CIA, didn't give a damn about.

Chapter 36: Unfinished Business

Bill Lair was not done with Laos, or Thailand, quite yet. Almost overnight Southeast Asia went from being the key to America's Anti-Communist campaign to an unmentionable backwater that no Washington policy maker dared touch after 1975. It was consigned to oblivion and remained there for a more than two decades with nothing emerging from it that caught national attention but a few ridiculously fictional films and 'Hollywood History' Rambo-esque superheroes. In 1992, 16 years after he retired from the Agency, it called upon Bill to use his Asian expertise to evaluate the situation in Cambodia where a Vietnamese satellite government headed by Hanoi's handpicked man Hun Sen continued to fight a low level anti-guerilla war against remnants of the Khmer Rouge. A war which had been going on for nearly 20 years. Langley wanted to know if it might be a good idea to fund a paramilitary force like the one Bill had raised in Laos to harass the Communists and gather intelligence. He took a trip to Thailand to check things out; returned to say it wouldn't be a good idea.

Over the years Bill's anger over what happened in Laos cooled. His hatred of Ted Shackley and Bill Sullivan, the leaders of America's Charge of the Light Brigade in Laos, faded. He gradually became more interested in the Hmong and other Lao refugees who came to America than those who stayed behind. He began to come out of his self-imposed shell. He began to be honored by the Hmong in America. He travelled to visit Vang Pao in Montana, to be honored ceremonially by the large Hmong communities in Minnesota and Wisconsin and California. The shy man of few words put himself forward to publicly support their culture and their cause. He had worried that the Hmong would become dependent on American aid in Laos. Worried about the same thing in the States.

Maybe he worried too much about them. Some Hmong did become dependent on Welfare for years. Their transition to American life was difficult, but not impossible. Those born in Laos had a particularly tough time, as the first wave of any immigrant group does, but their American born children and grandchildren have done well. And the old folks brought a toughness and independence with them that stood them in good stead in their new land. Many hit American ground, started gardening, and are still at it, virtually taking over the farmers' markets of Minneapolis and St. Paul; hard at work in the sprawling vegetable fields of California's Central Valley. You'll find them in places you might not expect to find them. Places like Walnut Grove, Minnesota, population 871, one of the small, shrinking struggling-to-survive towns in Southwestern Minnesota where 160-acre homesteads have been supplanted by 2,000-acre factory farms.

Walnut Grove's single claim to fame is that it was the home of Laura Ingalls Wilder which she used as setting for her *Little House on the Prairie.* My wife, Somsy, a Thai Isan peasant from a poor little village about the same size as Walnut Grove loves the TV show. It reminds her of her own youth. We visited the Wilder museum there not long ago and she was in ecstasy. While we were there a busload of elementary school children came in. Most of them were Hmong. According to the 2010 Census 300 of Walnut Grove's 871 people are Asian. I'll bet they're all Hmong. And I'd be willing to bet that a majority of people under the age of 50 in a number of other small struggling Southwestern Minnesota towns are also Hmong. They came because there were many big old (and cheap) houses in these dying towns that fit their big extended families. Houses that they can fix up and live comfortably in. They came to fill the kind of dirty, sweaty, often seasonal, jobs that the big farms have trouble filling. But most of all they came for the land. Even a few acres of rich black Minnesota soil is enough for them to grow a cornucopia of produce, raise some hogs and chickens, and bring back part of their old life in Laos, even if it is now on flat prairie land. Somsy and I are market gardeners too. It's not something we do because we want to make a lot of money, but it's pleasant exercise and good for the soul. And a good place to meet Hmong and hear their stories. So, the next time you think about life on the banks of Plum Creek try making the Ingalls family Hmong. That's more accurate these days.

Part VIII: Return of the Ancient Agent - 1992-2014

Chapter 37: Laos, Gone, but not Completely Forgotten

For more than 30 years after the Communist takeover of Laos little was heard about it in the USA. For the first 17 of those years it was the equivalent of a hermit kingdom. Off limits to everyone from the non-Communist world; not of much interest to the Communists, other than the Vietnamese and Chinese, either. Some stories leaked out. It was hard to tell if they were fact or fiction. There was no way to verify them. Stories of American prisoners still held in bamboo cages deep in its jungles. Stories of CIA-backed, or diehard Hmong, guerilla warriors still fighting the Communists; stories of rogue Americans sneaking into Laos to fight commies and rescue American POWs. Most of these stories can easily be dismissed as fantasy, either made for Hollywood or made up by con men raising money to fund their heroic supposed undertakings. But there were some stories that have the ring of truth to them though they cannot be verified.

There **were** Hmong who stayed behind in Laos. Nobody knows how many. There is no doubt that the occupying NVA wanted to annihilate them. They had been trying to do so for decades. The Hmong hid in the limestone karst mountains of Sayaboury Province and other of the most remote parts of what had been Hmong Country; sheltered in caves, drank from underground rivers, became masters of underground passageways. Barely survived by hunting and gathering and gardening. But when their gardens and slash-and-burn rice fields were discovered by the Lao government, as they inevitably were, they had to move on, had to flee to a new spot of deep jungle where they could hang on for another season, or two, before fleeing again. The Vietnamese were indiscriminate in their slaughter of the Hmong. They killed any Hmong they could get their hands on, even the Sayaboury native Hmong who'd never supported Vang Pao and had never fought against them. Killed them with any weapons at their disposal including poison gas. Killed and kept killing on into the 21st Century. Their unending campaign the very textbook example of genocide. A few Hmong continued to trickle out of Laos decades after the Communist takeover bearing tales of their people's plight that few non-Hmong listened to. Nobody except the Hmong who had fled Laos wanted to do anything about that plight.

Some tried to do something. They formed their own groups in the US to champion the cause of their people still in Laos. Many of them were groups of Hmong veterans. Few Americans were interested in the plight of the left-behind Hmong. Few knew anything about the Secret War in Laos. Our government gave them no encouragement. But by the year 2000 some people, both Hmong and American, were starting to take an interest in the deliberately forgotten Vietnam War and the even more forgotten Secret War in Laos.

Bill Lair, who had been effectively exiled from the CIA since his 1976 retirement, except for his brief 1992 consultation as a Cambodia expert, was brought back to Langley to address the graduates of the CIA Basic Class of 2000. A couple of years after that, following the 9/11 tragedy, his Operation Momentum paramilitary war principles were being widely discussed in Washington policy think tanks. Some thought they should be applied in Afghanistan, and for a while it looked like they would be. But it didn't happen despite some early experimentation. Soon the Green Berets and Special Forces and regular military guys sheep-dipped as civilian advisors showed up just like they did in Laos. Americans stuck out like a sore thumb as much in Afghanistan as they did in Laos. The Afghan Army and Police had to be trained and retrained, equipped and re-equipped, just like the RLA. It was the P.E.O. and the White Star Teams all over again. The American Way of War had a few new high-tech wrinkles; some like unmanned drones were even quite effective, but for the most part the playbook was the same as it had been in the 1960s-70s. Which meant that the results were pretty much the same too.

Another new wrinkle to US war strategy was more political than military. In 2006 the George W. Bush Administration adopted a program designed to seek out and attack terrorists while their attacks were still in the planning stages. It put our Federal Prosecutors on the front lines of the War on Terrorism. Wannabe terrorists would be caught before they could do their foul deeds and locked up for life to prevent them from ever doing any damage. Sounded like a good deal after 9/11 and the Islamist terror attacks that followed.

One of those Federal Prosecutors in California decided that there were Hmong terrorists lurking about as well. There wasn't much to support his supposition of Hmong terrorism, but there were a few stray things. There had been some "refugee politics" talk in the Hmong Community over the years of going back to Laos and winning the lost war; of aiding those few who were said to be still fighting it. Talk and rumor and wishful thinking speculation. Dreams of heroic actions that never got off the ground. Since there was no firm evidence our bold terrorist fighting prosecutor decided to make some up. He uncovered a silly Hollywood Action Movie plot hatched by a spaced-out New Age self-styled Lawrence of Arabia, a retired US Army Colonel named Harrison Jack. Perhaps he was a relative of the celluloid Billy Jack. The Colonel had attracted a group of nine mostly elderly naïve Hmong with a plan to stage a coup to overthrow the Communist government of Laos. His script lacked details, so our Fightin' Prosecutor helpfully supplied them.

He even sent a man 'round to try to sell arms to the wannabe Rambos. They seemed interested but had a problem. Colonel Jack's plan to raise money for his coup had flopped. Nobody wanted to buy the "kinetically charged" bottled water he was trying to sell to finance it. He'd have to try something else because his mystic girlfriend had consulted her crystal ball and told him that the Fightin' Prosecutor's bogus arms dealer was legit. There were no further meetings. No arms sale as the plotters didn't have enough money to buy any arms. No clandestine trip to Thailand in preparation for the "coup". Nothing. But that was enough as far as our legal beagle hero was concerned.

In January of 2007 Colonel Jack and his nine Hmong "accomplices" were arrested in Sacramento on charges of fomenting a "Terrorist Plot to murder thousands and thousands of people and overthrow the Laotian

Government". And, just for good measure, Vang Pao was arrested in Montana as having ordered the plot, even though he had no connection with the plotters. In June of that same year formal charges were laid against "the plotters". In July thousands of Hmong demonstrators turned out in front of the Sacramento Courthouse when the 11 men had their bail hearings. Vang Pao was devastated, never was himself again after the charges and hearings. Two of the elderly Hmong "co-conspirators" suffered strokes. If found guilty they all faced double-life terms plus 38 years. In September 2007 charges against Vang Pao were dropped. Though considered an evil genius by the anti-war left VP had friends on the far right, and some of those friends were well placed in the Bush Administration. The other 10 didn't have any non-Hmong friends except Bill Lair.

The case of the *United States vs Jack et al* did not come to trial for another three years. Meanwhile the terrorist fighting Federal Prosecutor hyped his lurid imaginative allegations vigorously. Bill was called on by their defense lawyer as an expert witness to debunk the Prosecutor's wild charges. He in turn gathered a few of his old Momentum team to help him out. Together the 86-year-old Lair and his almost as old buddies drafted an affidavit that soundly debunked every detail of the Prosecutor's charges as fabricated, distorted and witlessly fictional concluding that "this was not a serious plan by any stretch of the imagination". The trial finally began in October 2010. When the Prosecutor rolled out the fiendish plot supporting his charges Bill and his old spook buddies could hardly keep straight faces. The plotters would not only buy weapons, including heavy weapons and stinger missiles, from their friendly crystal-ball approved fake arms dealer, they'd hire a fearsome crew of soldier of fortune mercenaries. Then it would be off to Bangkok with their clanking carloads of ordnance and mercenary shock troops. Thence on to Vientiane where they'd kill those promised thousands and thousands and overthrow the government of the Peoples Democratic Republic of Laos.

The trial itself was as much comic opera as anything out of Gilbert and Sullivan, though with the lives and reputations of ten people at stake it was much more serious. The Hmong 10's defense lawyer had earlier called the

Federal Prosecutor's case "outrageous conduct by the government" and had no trouble proving that right. During the trial he called his own defendant Harrison Jack "a fool" only to have him prove conclusively what a fool he was under the Prosecutor's angry cross examination. Bill stood by ready to be called as a defense witness, but the prosecution was such a farce that his testimony wasn't needed. The presiding Judge suggested that the Prosecutor had no case but that failed to shut him up. On January 11, 2011 The *United States vs Jack et al* was dismissed. The Federal Government had spent more than ten million dollars pursuing the luckless "Hmong Terrorists". Uncle Sam was an even bigger fool than Harrison Jack. Vang Pao died five days before the dismissal was announced, a broken man.

Chapter 38 - Still More Fools

During the same time that octogenarian Bill Lair was fighting US Federal fools in California he was also doing battle with US and Thai fools in Southeast Asia. In truth, they weren't so much fools as they were uninformed or misinformed or didn't-want-be-informed bureaucratic deadheads. A narrow distinction to be sure. This was the across-the-pond end of same thing that underlay the furor in California. The plight of the "Jungle Hmong" still struggling to survive in Laos and those among them who had given up the struggle and fled to a Thailand that was no longer a haven for them. With Bill on this crusade was author Roger Warner who, among other things, wrote the best, most comprehensive, and most accurate history of the Secret War in Laos, *Shooting at the Moon (1996)*. The two of them arrived in Bill's old stomping ground of Nong Khai in 2007 to interview 150 Jungle Hmong who were being held in a Thai Detention Center there. Another 8,000 Jungle Hmong were also being held in a Thai refugee camp. The Thais wanted to boot the whole lot of them back across the Mekong to Laos. They blandly called their plan "Repatriation". The Hmong in the US and some Americans called it "Murder". Murder, or death by imprisonment, starvation and forced labor, was the likely outcome of any "repatriation". The Communist government of Laos expressed no interest in the Thai plan. Offered no guarantees of the safety of any "repatriates".

Bill gently interviewed the prisoners in Nong Khai. They had been separated from the other Jungle Hmong because the Thais believed them to be former Vang Pao soldiers. With his customary tact and patience Bill found out that the Thais were right. They were Hmong soldiers. Most of them boy soldiers from the waning days of the war. In their 50's now, made older than their years by the harsh life they'd led; many still bearing the scars of their youthful service. One of them was Blia Shou Herr who had hung on in Laos until government troops killed his wife while she was foraging for food in 2006. One of his sons lived in Sacramento and was a US citizen. With no kin left alive in Laos he longed to join him. Soon after Blia arrived at the Detention Center the Thais tried to dump him and the other detainees on the far side of the Mekong. They barricaded themselves in their cells and threatened mass suicide saying that that would be better than what awaited them in Laos. The Thais backed off and began to treat them even more viciously than they'd been treating before in hopes that they'd change their minds.

Bill and Roger went back to Bangkok and had an audience with US Ambassador Eric C. John who oozed tactful sympathy for the plight of the Jungle Hmong and palmed them off on his man in charge of refugee affairs who was supposedly acquainted with Thai General Niphat Thonglek, the man in charge of the "Hmong Repatriation Program". Turns out his only contact with the General was a few days spent flying around southern Thailand in a chopper surveying Tsunami damage in 2004. Bill asked him if he had asked Niphat about Hmong repatriation and he said no. When asked why not he replied, "He wasn't at my level". A few years later General Niphat became Thailand's Defense Minister. Bill was livid at this pompous Foreign Service ass. He recalled the old days when many US Ambassadors and their staffers had the common touch, behaved like they were from the United States, not from the upper crust of Victorian England.

Their supercilious host led them on a tour of the US Hmong resettlement operation at Wat Tam Krabok near Lopburi, site of Bill's first assignment in Thailand in 1951. Bill chatted in Thai, Lao and Hmong with the "refugees" there. Then came back and told his host that they were Hmong, but they weren't refugees. That they had never been in Laos. That their people had been in Thailand for centuries. Something they freely admitted to him as he was the first person they'd ever talked to who knew their language and their culture. They were just looking for a free trip to "the golden mountain" America. He didn't blame them for trying. Lots of other fake refugees and asylum seekers were trying to game the US immigration system. None of the Americans working in the program spoke their language. All were believers in the purity and noble suffering of refugees. What a mess. A US Embassy that ignores real Hmong refugees in desperate need while it packs hundreds of fake refugees who're playing the system off to America.

With no help from US or Thai officialdom Bill sought out some of his old Thai contacts but they couldn't, or wouldn't, help him. Most were now retired. Those who weren't lived in fear of crossing the younger men now jockeying for power. Thailand's never placid military politics were more poisonous than usual. The Thais closed the "unauthorized" refugee camp at Wat Tam Krabok and the US transported its fake Hmong refugees to America. During December of 2009 5000 Thai Army and Police were deployed to "round up troublemakers" and force 4000 real Hmong refugees from a camp at Nam Khao in remote Phetchabun Province across the border into Laos. They cut off medical and food aid provided by civilian agencies before their operation "to bring them under control". The Thai spokesman for the repatriation said that the refugees "will be well treated in Laos"; where there are still reports of genocidal attacks on the Hmong. The US and UN mildly objected to the repatriation. A State Department Official vaguely suggested that the US might admit some of the Hmong as asylum seekers but did nothing beyond that. As of December 29, 2009, the 150 Jungle Hmong Bill and Roger visited at Nong Khai were still in detention and scheduled for repatriation. They have not been heard from since. There may be as many as 4,000 more Hmong refugees facing repatriation.

Bill and Roger returned to the US having accomplished nothing.

Chapter 39 – The End 2014

Bill Lair continued to be honored by the Hmong during his last few years on earth. Frail but still clear of mind and game he made several trips to St. Paul, Minnesota and Eau Claire, Wisconsin at their invitation. One of those trips was covered by a local television station. While awaiting the appearance of a speaker at the podium their reporter interviewed several people in the crowd asking them about the significance of the three larger-than-life paintings that provided a backdrop for the speaker. He knew that the center picture was of General Vang Pao and that the picture on the left was of the King of Laos, but he didn't know who the American in the picture on the right was. The young Hmong he asked didn't know who he was either. Finally, he asked an old soldier in full uniform.

"That's Bill Lair, the best American friend the Hmong ever had." He replied.

There's a youtube video of Bill's last public appearance on July 4, 2014 in St. Paul in honor of his 90th birthday. He makes his way slowly to the podium, but under his own power. Speaks slowly but clearly standing almost straight, his wrists bulging with the *baci* strings of Hmong who wish to tie their souls to his great soul. On October 28 of that same year James William Lair dies in The Colony, Texas, a Dallas suburb where his daughter Lehta still lives. Later his body is interred in Arlington National Cemetery.

Afterword

My book writing career began at age 65 in the little village of Nong Lak thirty miles east of Udorn. I had spent much of my several adult careers writing translations and situation reports at Ramasun, writing Requirements Analyses and operating manuals and Requests for Proposals in my next incarnation as a Computer Systems Analyst and Software Developer; but never had I done any creative writing. The writing I'd done before 2010 wasn't supposed to be creative.

My wife Somsy and I had been spending winters in her village in Thailand for some years. Nong Lak is a quiet unexciting place where we are surrounded by the Thai side of our blended family. I had been doing a lot of reading when one day it dawned on me that, at age 65, maybe I should be adding to the literary pot. I tried writing a few short stories about the village, which I liked though I didn't think they were quite up to snuff. Then, on one of my daily early morning hikes around the lake (Nong = Lake), a story came to me that I really liked. A story about Ramasun Station. I scribbled it down before the afternoon heat built up. Liked it so well that I kept on writing until I ran out of paper. Went to the nearby district town on Nong Han and got some from a shop that sold school supplies; 50-page wide-lined notebooks with a pirated picture of "Hello Kitty" on the cover identified as "My Little Kittie"; a humble start to my writing career.

Got a few a of my stories published in collections and anthologies, then decided to combine the best of them in a short story collection. Naturally no one wanted to publish it so I self-published on Amazon's Create Space. Their software was crappy but being a computer nerd, I could handle it. It's much better now. Hence *Tales of Ramasun* was born in 2012. I eventually had enough stories to fill two sequels, then decided to take a crack at historical fiction with a novel set in my native Minnesota during the Dakota War of 1862 titled *Dacotah Blood* and a novel set in Minnesota and Laos during the Secret War titled *Mysterious Mike and the Hmong*. They were harder to write because they required research, but I loved doing the work. None of my books are best sellers. The *Ramasun* books chug modestly along. It's too early to tell about the others.

Then, one day about two years ago, I discovered Bill Lair. I was amazed that I hadn't heard of him. Our paths had crossed. I arrived at Ramasun Station a few months after he left the nearby Udorn Airbase in 1968. Left Thailand a few months after he returned to Bangkok in 1970. He may have read some of the translations and Sitreps (situation reports) I wrote. My best Lao "lingy" Army buddy grew up near Panhandle, TX and knew that country, but not Bill. I started out just wanting to find out more about him and, as a I found more, I started thinking about writing something about him. Thinking in terms of another historical fiction book. In doing more research I was unable to find either a Bill Lair autobiography, or biography. But could I write one? It looked too scholarly for me. Finally, I decided to give it a whack. What the hell! I wrote my original *Tales of Ramasun* because I couldn't find any books about Ramasun Station. I'd write a Bill Lair biography because there wasn't a Bill Lair biography.

It hasn't been easy. The easy part came first. I used Ancestry.com to trace Bill's family tree and found lots of interesting stuff. Just like the great stuff I'd found tracing my own family tree a few years earlier. I knew how to take the genealogy I found and hunt for background on the Internet. Then it was on to the tough stuff. I found plenty on Bill, but it was buried in many books and articles and websites and files. Some of it was vague. Some of it was contradictory. Some of it turned out to be just plain wrong. The worst part of the whole exercise was establishing a timeline for Bill's life. Much of the information I found wasn't attached to dates. In some cases, it was attached to dates I later found to be wrong. What happened, when, and in what order was a continual nightmare. There's no official history of the CIA's Secret War in Laos or of Bill's PARU days in Thailand to fall back on. There probably never will be.

In the end all I can say is the same thing Bill said about his efforts in Southeast Asia...I just figure that I did the best I could.

And I had some help. My sister Rebecca Stanton assisted me with graphics, maps and artwork, as well as genealogy searching. My wife Somsy provided inspiration in addition to a long-running education on Thailand and its people. I drew background information from many Hmong and Lao friends and acquaintances in Minnesota. I've had the time of my old life writing this book and I hope those who read it will find the truth-is-stranger-than-fiction life of James William Lair interesting and inspirational.

References:

Books

Ahern, Thomas L Jr: *Vietnam Declassified: The CIA and Counterinsurgency,* University of Kentucky Press: Lexington, 2012.

Blaufarb, Douglas S: *The Counterinsurgency Era: U.S. Doctrine and Performance 1950 to the Present,* Macmillan: New York, 1977.

Castle, Timothy N: *At War in the Shadow of Vietnam: U. S. Military Aid to the Royal Lao Government 1955-75,* Columbia University Press: New York, 1993.

Conboy, Kenneth, with James Morrison: *Shadow War: The CIA's Secret War in Laos,* Paladin Press: Boulder CO, 1995.

Corn, David: *Blond Ghost,* Simon & Schuster: New York, 1994.

Curry, Robert: *Whispering Death: Our Journey with the Hmong in the Secret War for Laos,* IUniverse: New York, 2004.

Dakin, Bret: *Another Quiet American: Stories of Life in Laos,* Asia Books, Bangkok, 2003.

Hathorn, Reginald: *Here There are Tigers: The Secret Air War in Laos.* Stackpole: Mechabnicsburg VA, 2008.

Kurlantzick, Joshua: *A Great Place to Have a War: America in Laos and the Birth of a Military CIA.* Simon and Schuster: New York, 2016.

Meeker, Oden: *The Little World of Laos:* Charles Scribner's Sons: New York, 1959.

Meritt, Jane Hamilton: *Tragic Mountains: The Hmong, the Americans, and the Secret War in Laos, 1942-92.* Indiana University Press: Bloomington, 1999.

Parker, James E: *Codename Mule: Fighting the Secret War in Laos for the CIA.* Naval Institute Press: Annapolis MD, 1995.

Robbins, Christopher: *The Ravens: The Men Who Flew in America's Secret War in Laos.* Crown: New York, 1987.

Robbins, Christopher: *Air America: The Story of the CIA's Secret Airlines.* Putnam: New York, 1979.

Schanche, Don A: *Mister Pop: The Adventures of a Peaceful Man in a Small War.* David McKay: New York, 1970.

Secord, Richard: *Honored and Betrayed: Irangate, Covert Affairs, and the Secret War in Laos.* John Wiley and Sons: New York, 1992.

Stevenson, Charles A: *The End of Nowhere: American Policy Toward Laos Since 1954.* Beacon Press: Boston, 1972.

Warner, Roger: *Shooting at the Moon: The Story of America's Clandestine War in Laos.* Steerforth Press: South Royalton, VT, 1996.

Webb, Billy G: *The Secret War in Laos and General Vang Pao 1958-1975.* Xlibrism.com, 2016.

Weldon, Charles, M.D.: *Tragedy in Paradise: A Country Doctor at War in Laos.* Asian Books: Bangkok, 1999.

Young, Gordon: *Tracks of an Intruder*: Travsin Publications, Bangkok, 1991.

Online Websites and Articles Available Online

Ancestry.com.: Census, family tree, marriage, school, military and death records.

Army War College website, armywarcollege.edu.

Huffpost.com

Hutchinson County (TX) Boomtown Museum, Borger TX website.

Minneapolis Star Tribune, articles

St. Paul Pioneer Press, articles.

Suab Hmong Broadcasting, youtube.com.

Suab Hmong News, shrdo.com.

Texas A & M University website, tamu.edu.

Veterans Archive Project, Texas Tech University, Lubbock: 8-20-2010 Interview with 86-year-old Bill Lair covering his early life and WWII service by Ellen Hurst.

Veterans Archive Project, Texas Tech University, Lubbock: 12-11-2001 Interview with 77-year-old Bill Lair Part 1 covering his childhood and education to December 1942, WWII service to 11/45 by Steve Maxner.

Veterans Archive Project, Texas Tech University, Lubbock: 12-11-2001 Interview with 77-year-old Bill Lair Part 2 covering his education 1945-49 and CIA career 1949-76 by Steve Maxner.

Warner, Roger, 2011 series of articles under title *Strange New Life of a Secret War* in Huffpost.

Wikipedia. Com. The place to start for leads to other information.

Youtube.com. 2010 Video from Vietnam Archives of 2010 biographical Interview of Bill Lair.

Youtube.com. Videos of Bill Lair 2013 to 2015. Interviews with Hmong news In St. Paul, Lacrosse, Sacramento and at Arlington National Cemetery. Honored on 89th and 90th Birthdays. Honored upon his death in 2014, and one year after his death in 2015.

Youtube.com. 1980 Video of interview with Vint Lawrence.

Made in the USA
Columbia, SC
18 September 2020

20999041R00124